INSIDE CAMELOT

BEN BRADLEE, executive editor of the *Washington Post,* was a close personal friend of the Kennedys from 1959 until JFK's death in 1963. He was one of the few who saw the First Family "off duty"—Jackie defending $40,000 in department-store bills, explaining a cruise aboard Aristotle Onassis' yacht, and calling her husband "Bunny;" JFK playing with his children, balancing the family budget (or trying to), gossiping with J. Edgar Hoover, watching his wife on TV with pride and a touch of jealousy, learning the twist from Lee Radziwill, and leaking items to *Newsweek* (Bradlee was Washington bureau chief of *Newsweek* at the time).

"This is John F. Kennedy as his best friends remember him—'half the "mick" politician . . . half the bright, graceful, intellectual *Playboy of the Western World.*'" —*Newsweek*

CONVERSATIONS WITH KENNEDY
was originally published by W. W. Norton & Company, Inc.

Conversations
WITH *Kennedy*

Benjamin C. Bradlee

Illustrated with photographs

PUBLISHED BY POCKET BOOKS NEW YORK

CONVERSATIONS WITH KENNEDY

W. W. Norton edition published 1975

POCKET BOOK edition published May, 1976

This POCKET BOOK edition includes every word contained in
the original, higher-priced edition. It is printed from brand-
new plates made from completely reset, clear, easy-to-read type.
POCKET BOOK editions are published by
POCKET BOOKS,
a division of Simon & Schuster, Inc.,
A GULF+WESTERN COMPANY
630 Fifth Avenue,
New York, N.Y. 10020.
Trademarks registered in the United States
and other countries.

1276

For his "god-child," Marina,
and his friend, Dino

Introduction

THIS IS a record of conversations I had with John F. Kennedy during the five years that I knew him—between 1959, when he was a senator running for president, and 1963, when he died on the 1007th day of his presidency.

From the day I met him—I think it was in a Senate corridor after President Eisenhower's state of the union message in January, 1959—through the first year of his presidency, I kept no formal notes of these conversations. During that time I was first a political reporter in the Washington bureau of *Newsweek* magazine, and later its bureau chief. In those capacities, I wrote hundreds of thousands of words, many of them about Kennedy, many of them about conversations with Kennedy, many on the record, and many off the record. I have used these files to refresh my memory, in writing about conversations during this period.

But Kennedy's impact on me as a person, and as a journalist lately come to the glamor of Washington, was so strong—and remains so even today, fifteen years later—that I can still quote verbatim whole chunks of conversations with him.

It is this powerful impact which accounts for the absence of a formal record of our conversations during the first years of our friendship. It happens to very few of us that some neighbor, some family friend, someone whose children play with your children (however reluctantly), becomes president of the United States.

INTRODUCTION

It now seems clear that when it happened to me, that friendship dominated my life, as Walter Lippmann had warned me it could. It was invaluable to me as a journalist, of course, and I used it without embarrassment to give *Newsweek* the intimate details of the life and thinking of this remarkable man who lit the skies of this land bright with hope and promise as no other political man has done in this century.

And even though *Newsweek* could run only small portions of what I was writing about President Kennedy every week, for a time those small portions satisfied my hunger to contribute to the recording of contemporary history.

But then there came a time when that hunger was no longer satisfied. There came a time when I understood that I had a unique, historical access to this fascinating man. Not the access of those who worked so closely with him and created with him the public record—the Bundys, the Sorensens, the O'Donnells, the O'Briens, the McNamaras. Nor the access of those many who had known him longer and better. But the unique access of a journalist who saw him after the day's work was done, who saw him relaxed and anxious for companionship and diversion, eager to interrupt his sobering duties with conversation, gossip, and laughter. And I knew enough of history to know that the fruits of this kind of access seldom make the history books, and the great men of our time are less understood as a result.

It was then that I started keeping detailed records of conversations, telephone calls, and contacts with JFK. These records were normally dictated into a machine within twenty-four hours after they took place. The nature of these contacts varied enormously—from one- or two-minute telephone calls, to weekends at Palm Beach, Newport, or Camp David. Their frequency varied equally—from three times in four days, or five times a month, to zero times in three months. My notes of these conversations and contacts were taken with President Kennedy's knowledge, and with the understanding only that they would not be published without his permission for at least five years after he left the White House. In fact, I did not look at these notes for ten years after he died.

It is stating the obvious that the sum total of all these contacts—somewhere between 125 to 150 over a period of five years—is neither numerically nor qualitatively sufficient to constitute anything like complete understanding of a vital and complicated man, who had lived so much of his life before I ever knew him. And it is equally obvious that since the setting of these contacts was predominantly social, the President Kennedy that I saw and heard in the flesh was a president off duty, a president trying to relax, a president in search of personal contact otherwise denied him by the burdens and isolation of his lonely office.

And so the portrait is necessarily personal and one-dimensional, reflecting only what Kennedy said to me —not what he said to others—reflecting generally what he said and did after hours—not what he said and did when he was actually presiding over the crises and tensions of the country. And surely reflecting my personality, not the personality of someone with a different sense of values, humor, and proportion, whose conversations with Kennedy would be essentially different.

This record is sprinkled with what some will consider vulgarity. They may be shocked. Others, like Kennedy and like myself, whose vocabularies were formed in the crucible of life in the World War II Navy in the Pacific Ocean, will understand instinctively. There is nothing inherently vulgar in the legendary soldier's description of a broken-down Jeep. "The fucking fucker's fucked." Surely, there is no more succinct, or even graceful, four-word description of that particular state of affairs. I never heard Kennedy tell a dirty joke, and I never saw in him the true vulgarities of contempt.

Journalism is just the first rough draft of history, the late Philip Graham once said to emphasize the reality that journalists never could know the whole truth right away. The whole truth takes too long to emerge, and it consists of too many strands for a single journalist to catch in the single sitting that daily journalism demands. This record of conversations is the whole and unchanged truth—about those conversations, but all together the conversations made up only a few, if essential, strands of the whole truth that was John Kennedy.

"What makes journalism so fascinating," President Kennedy once said to me, "and biography so interesting [is] the struggle to answer that single question: 'What's he like?"

Well, John F. Kennedy was like this . . . at the times and places we saw each other. Eleven years ago, I described him as graceful, gay, funny, witty, teasing and teasable, forgiving, hungry, incapable of being corny, restless, interesting, interested, exuberant, blunt, profane, and loving. He was all of those . . . and more.

His brief time in power seems to me now to have been filled more with hope and promise than performance. But the hope and the promise that he held for America were real, and they have not been approached since his death.

"Seldom Seen"
Forks of Capon, West Virginia

November, 1974

Conversations
WITH *Kennedy*

Gaps in the Record

THERE ARE TWO significant gaps in this record of conversations with John F. Kennedy, one major, about thirty-six months, one minor, about three months, both important for their implications about the relations between the press and the presidency, and specifically between this reporter and that president.

If my five-year relationship with Kennedy had been purely personal, there probably would have been no gaps, and no written record. If this relationship had been purely professional, there may have been gaps, but there would exist a complete record.

To any man, but especially to a journalist, it is exciting to consider the prospect that a friend and a neighbor might, just possibly, become president of the United States. But it is also vaguely rattling, leading as it does to both subjective and objective considerations of the candidate's talents that normal voters don't make. Living in Europe as I had from 1951 to 1957, I had no firsthand knowledge of the two campaigns that had set the stage for the 1960 presidential elections. I had missed most of the Joe McCarthy period, and all of its national political fallout. I had missed both Stevenson campaigns, and therefore was unfamiliar and uncomfortable with the hold he had on the minds of most of my colleagues and most of my liberal friends. I had not been around to watch the rebirth of the Republican Party under Eisenhower after twenty years of Democratic rule. Most particu-

President Kennedy, attentive host to Tony Bradlee in Hyannisport. We waited there through the night and well into the next day for the election returns and the final verdict. "I now wanted Kennedy to win. I wanted my friend and neighbor to be president. . . . When Illinois finally put him over the top, Tony and I got a message asking us to come over to the Kennedys' for supper. . . . Over dinner he told us how he had called Chicago's Mayor Richard Daley while Illinois was hanging in the balance to ask how he was doing. 'Mr. President,' Kennedy quoted Daley as saying, 'With a little bit of luck and the help of a few close friends, you're going to carry Illinois.' Later, . . . I often wondered about that statement."

larly as far as Kennedy was concerned, I had missed JFK's brief and abortive emergence as a national political figure when he tried for the vice-presidency with Stevenson in 1956. And so when I first got to know Kennedy well, no historical precedents inhibited me when I first wondered if he might make president. It seemed so unlikely, if only because one's friends didn't (then) even run for president, much less get elected. Early on, my wife and I often said to him how strange it was for us that he should be a presidential candidate, and asked him often if it didn't seem strange to him. "Yes," he once replied, "until I stop and look around at the other people who are running for the job. And then I think I'm just as qualified as they are."

I remember once, toward the end of 1959, asking him, "Do you really think—way down deep—that you can pull this thing off?" And he paused, for a long time, which was not characteristic, and said quietly: "Yes, if I don't make a single mistake myself, and if I don't get maneuvered into a position where there is no way out." He said he meant by this that he could never finish second in a primary, never get into a situation like the one Stassen got into with Dewey in the Oregon primary of 1948 where everything was riding on a single event, and then blow that.

I'm not sure now that I believed him then. I was working overtime to overcome my lack of political knowledge, but I knew too much already to trust my political judgments and not enough to trust my political hunches. My uncertainties were quickly tested in the primaries. He ran up a record vote in the first of these primaries—in New Hampshire—but he was running there against the west wind, against a political unknown. And in Wisconsin, he never admitted it publicly but he ran substantially behind what he had privately predicted. On the day Wisconsin voters went to the polls, he flew to some town in northern Michigan in the *Caroline* for a midday political rally before coming back for the returns, and I went with him. During the flight I asked him for his prediction in each of the ten Wisconsin election districts. He wouldn't tell me, but agreed to write them down and put them in a sealed envelope, if I would do the same. We did, and Kennedy put them casually in a drawer on the plane, and switched the subject. Two or three days later, I was back on assignment on the Kennedy family plane and remembered the envelope. He pulled it out and showed me the predictions. I had put down "Kennedy 7, Humphrey 3," out of an abundance of caution; I really thought it would be eight to two. Kennedy himself had put down "JFK 9, HHH 1." But he actually carried only six districts to Humphrey's four, and I was obviously influenced by the disparity between our predictions and the actual outcome.

Maybe I had communicated some of my doubts to the editors of *Newsweek,* although they had plenty of their own, having covered many more presidential elections. Once I arranged to have Kennedy meet with these editors for dinner at the Links Club in New York, and later with some of the editors at the home of my friend, Blair Clark, then a CBS news executive. They gave him the hardest of times, slamming questions at him, obviously skeptical of the chances of a man who was too young, too Catholic, too eastern, too urbane. Crusty Hal Lavine, who had been covering presidential campaigns for *Newsweek* before Kennedy was a junior congressman, asked him what he was going to do that would convince the skeptics, what could he pull off that would impress the skeptics that he wasn't "just another pretty boy from Boston and Harvard." Kennedy was enjoying himself, despite the heat he was getting, and he turned to Lavine and stopped him cold by saying, "Well, I'm going to fucking well take Ohio, for openers." Not only had none of the editors heard a presidential candidate express himself exactly that way, but all of them knew that taking Ohio would in fact impress the skeptics, and they were impressed with Kennedy's conviction.

That line never appeared in print. The press generally protected Kennedy, as they protected all candidates, from his excesses of language and his sometimes outspokenly deprecatory characterizations of other politicians. Kennedy sometimes referred to Lyndon Johnson, and truly without hostility, as a "riverboat gambler," and often as "Landslide," a reference to the time when LBJ was first elected to the Senate by a majority in the primary of eighty-seven votes. He liked Stuart Symington as a human being, and felt the 1960 Democratic convention would most likely turn to Symington if they stopped him, but he stood in less than awe of his intellectual ability and said so often and bluntly to reporters. Other politicians said the same thing about Kennedy, of course, but the press appreciated Kennedy for his openness and protected him, while the press reacted skeptically to other candidates.

Vice-President Nixon attracted at least as many reporters, many of them, including myself, who were spending most of their time covering Kennedy. The difference was the difference between night and day. In the first place, the men around Nixon, with the exceptions of Bob Finch, the campaign director, Herb Klein, then as later in charge of Nixon's press, and New York political operator Len Hall, when he was allowed into the Inner Sanctum, cordially disliked the press and simply spoke a different language, where the men around Kennedy genuinely liked the press and spoke the same language.

At any time during the Kennedy campaign, a reporter could get to Larry O'Brien, Ken O'Donnell, Ted Sorensen, Bobby, all of them, often for a drink, always for a bull session. During the Nixon campaign, it took an all-day siege to get a few minutes with the men around Nixon, and they made reporters feel like lepers during those few minutes. And of course, Kennedy himself genuinely liked reporters. Some of his best friends—as the saying goes—were in fact reporters. He even had been a newspaperman once, himself—as another saying goes. (He covered the San Francisco conference which founded the United Nations in 1945 for the Hearst syndicate.)

Kennedy loved to shoot the breeze with reporters. He knew about the politics of each newspaper and magazine, the political politics and the office politics. And he knew this instinctively, without briefings. Nixon, on the other hand, then as later, was plagued by his discomfort with the press. On the rare occasions when he tried to be "one of the boys," the boys and girls of the press felt he was putting on an act, as he was. And all of this, despite the fact that the Nixon press operation was far smoother than the Kennedy operation. On the Nixon press plane, there was order; press releases were issued in good time; schedules were issued well in advance, and adhered to rigidly. And the press grumbled, openly hoping for assignment to the JFK camp. On the Kennedy press plane there was informal, friendly chaos, and the press loved it. In short, Kennedy was stimulated by reporters; Nixon was annoyed by them.

It was—and is—all an elaborate, ritualistic mating

dance, this vital relationship between the press and presidential candidates and presidents. The whole purpose of a campaign from the point of view of the politicians is to give the press something favorable to write about the candidate, and the press is vaguely resentful of being so used. The whole purpose of the campaign from the point of view of the press is to get to know the candidate as he really is, not as his public relations operation says he is, and the candidate is vaguely resentful of being such a target. These are the rules, and they must be followed with complete understanding by both sides, and with as much humor as possible. It is not the great adversary relationship it is cracked up to be, provided these rules are understood.

A case in point involves crowd estimates, always a bone of contention between the press and the presidential candidate. Once the Kennedy apparatus had announced that some JFK rally had been attended by 35,000 people, a figure which seemed to the traveling reporters to be substantially high. I asked Kennedy how they arrived at that figure, and he said to me and half a dozen other reporters: "Plucky (press secretary Pierre Salinger's nickname) counts the nuns, and then multiplies them by 100." By so deprecating the crowd count, and making a joke about a subject that was sensitive, to say the least, Kennedy made the reporters laugh, and probably avoided a story about inflated crowd counts by his staff.

Questioning of a crowd count given the press by a member of the Nixon team usually brought a lecture about bias.

The major gap is in fact the absence of any intention to keep a written record of my contacts with JFK.

When I first realized that chance was going to give me a special access to this bright and graceful and witty man who hungered to have a special impact on his times, and who seemed to be coming closer to his goal every day, I naively saw no conflict of interest between friendship and journalism. I was not sure he would become that significant a historical figure, and I was completely ignorant of my ultimate access and relationship to him.

As best I can now remember, that first moment came on the afternoon of a sparkling late summer day in 1958. My wife and I had bumped into the Kennedys during an afternoon walk in Georgetown. Already casual acquaintances, they now were new neighbors. We talked then for an hour or so in their garden, a few doors from our house, and we drew each other as dinner partners later that night. The subject of those conversations—like so many that followed—was the private lives and public postures of politicians, reporters, and friends.

This major gap in my written record lasted until August, 1961, when I first recorded a meeting with Kennedy, but it really lasted longer—until February, 1962, when I started making a record of every meeting with him. A gap, then, of some three years, during which I was groping for the answer to a question that has plagued Washington journalists since the birth of the Republic: What is the dividing line between friendship and professionalism?* Closeness brings the access

---

* The most dramatic decision of this kind in my knowledge was thrust on Richard Harwood, then a *Washington Post* reporter, now editor of the Trenton, N.J., *Times,* in June of 1968, when he held the dying Robert Kennedy in his arms on the floor of the kitchen of the Ambassador Hotel in Los Angeles. Harwood had been assigned to cover Kennedy by me (perhaps because I knew something about the charm of

that is essential to understanding, but with closeness come potentially conflicting loyalties.

By 1960 I had been a cub reporter, a police reporter, a court reporter, a foreign correspondent, and a political reporter for fourteen years. I had spent a majority of these years outside Washington, in New Hampshire and in Paris. As a result, I had fewer politicians as friends than most of my colleagues and all of my competitors, and I worried about it. This thing I had going with the junior senator from Massachusetts was very seductive. He had the smell of success, and my special access to him was enormously valuable to *Newsweek,* in whose Washington bureau I was then working. And I truly liked him; our wives were becoming friends; we ate and drank together.

I never wrote less than I knew about him, filing the good with the bad. But obviously, the information Kennedy gave me tended to put him and his policies in a favorable light, even though all such information was passed through special filters, in the first instance by me, and to a greater extent by *Newsweek*'s editors. If I was had, so be it; I doubt I will ever be so close to a political figure again. If I should get that close again, there will be nothing missing from my record of conversations.

The minor gap in the record began in August, 1962, when *Look* magazine published an article by Fletcher Knebel entitled "Kennedy vs. The Press," and subtitled "Never have so few bawled out so many so often

politicians in general, and of Kennedys in particular) since he had been outspokenly skeptical of Bobby. But they had become friends. As Dick told it months later, "I looked down at that poor man with his head on my lap, and for thirty seconds I wondered, 'What the hell am I—a friend or a reporter?'" At the end of those agonizing seconds, Harwood called his office, his decision made in favor of journalism.

for so little, as the Kennedys battle reporters." In the light of the Nixon experience, and in light of the simple, historic fact that John Kennedy enjoyed better relations with the press than any president since Mergenthaler invented the linotype, the hyperbole here is hard to believe. But the immediate problem for me centered on two paragraphs in the story, plus some bit of graphic hyperbole by *Look*'s art director, entitled "They've Dueled With Kennedy" beneath an old woodcut of a bearded man in a three-quarter-length coat, left hand behind his back, right hand with pistol raised high at the ready.

The paragraphs at issue read as follows:

Even a good friend of the President, Benjamin C. Bradlee, Washington bureau chief of *Newsweek,* felt the presidential fire. Kennedy phoned him to take him to task for a *Newsweek* story about an old Massachusetts aide of Kennedy's being considered for a federal judgeship. Also ticked off later by Attorney General Kennedy for another story, Bradlee takes the rebukes philosophically and not too seriously.

"It's almost impossible," he says, "to write a story they like. Even if a story is quite favorable to their side, they'll find one paragraph to quibble with."

Would anyone believe I thought that quote was off the record? Anyway, I said it, and of course it was true. Kennedys by definition want 110 percent from their friends, especially their friends in the press, and feel cheated by anything less. I do remember Kennedy calling to complain about the "old Massachusetts aide." That was Francis Xavier Morrissey, a municipal (pronounced MU-ni-SIP-ple in Boston) court judge, whose legal abilities were taxed by parking ticket cases, and whom Kennedy was trying to slip unnoticed onto the federal bench. And I remember what the president of the United States said: "Jesus Christ, you guys are something else. When I was elected, you all said that my old man would run the country in consultation with the pope. Now here's the only thing he's ever asked me to do for him, and you guys piss all over me."

I have no recollection of the particular incident that ticked off the attorney general.*

The graphics included two boxes containing lists of names of journalists, one called "Jumped on by Jack," and the other "Bawled out by Bobby." My name was the only one to make both lists.†

---

* I did have my troubles with Robert F. Kennedy, notably in early 1964. One day I spent sixteen hours seated next to him, lined yellow pad on my lap and pencil flashing, starting in the gray of the morning at his home, flying to Kansas City and points west to dedicate a Catholic home for the aged, and ending up in New York City well after dark. The upshot of this day was a story under my byline in *Newsweek* saying that Bobby Kennedy wanted to be Lyndon Johnson's vice-president, which he did and which he said he did. The story made a lot of ink flow, as the French say, until President Johnson ruled out his entire cabinet as potential vice-presidents, thus manufacturing a formal excuse for not naming Bobby. When the story appeared in *Newsweek*, Kennedy's press secretary, Ed Guthman, first denied the story, claiming that I had not even seen Bobby. Later, in that most castrating of journalistic putdowns, he admitted we had seen each other, but claimed the whole conversation was off the record, which it was not. Later I came to have the greatest respect for Bobby Kennedy's commitment and compassion and ability.

† Others "Jumped on by Jack": Art Buchwald, the humorist; Garnett D. Horner, *Washington Evening Star;* Marianne Means, Hearst Headline Service; Hugh S. Sidey, *Time;* John Sutherland, *U.S. News & World Report.* Others "Bawled out by Bobby": Robert S. Allen and Roscoe Drummond, syndicated columnists; Earl Mazo, *New York Herald Tribune.*

This really irritated the president of the United States. Later he was to explain: "Jesus, there you are really plugged in, better than any other reporter except Charlie (Bartlett), getting one exclusive after another out of this place, and what do you do but dump all over us." To make matters worse, John Denson, editor of the *New York Herald Tribune,* latched on to the story and ordered the *Tribune*'s Washington bureau chief, Robert Donovan, to interview all of us historians in the doghouse. Hugh Sidey of *Time* had the good sense to bail out of trouble by saying that "the Kennedys may gripe a little but they are the best news sources in history." When Donovan called me, I felt I was already in hopelessly hot water with the Kennedys and was quoted only as saying that I declined to comment.

And that did it. From regular contact—dinner at the White House once and sometimes twice a week, and telephone calls as needed in either direction—to no contact. The next time we saw the Kennedys was in November, three months later, when Jackie invited my wife, Tony, and the children over for movies and lollipops. A few days later Kennedy and Tony were talking at a dance about how hard it was to be friends with someone who wrote everything he knew, and we were pals again.

It seems strange now, so many years later, that a friendship like ours could not survive such a minor irritant. Some of the reasons have their roots in that wonderful law of the Boston Irish political jungle: "Don't get mad; get even." He never got mad, but he plainly got even, cutting me out of a mainstream of information that had been enormously valuable to me and to *Newsweek.* At issue, then and later, was the question that plagued us both: What, in fact, was I?

A friend, or a journalist? I wanted to be both. And whereas I think Kennedy valued my friendship—I made him laugh, I brought him the fruits of contact with an outside world from which he was now shut out —he valued my journalism most when it carried his water.

To fill in these gaps, especially the long, first one, is hard now, fifteen years later. Some incidents have blurred, and without a contemporaneous record, my memory is suspect. Others are still remarkably vivid, and I could swear to the accuracy of my recollections, right down to long quotes from Kennedy.

The first of these vivid memories is of the night of the 1960 West Virginia primary, the first of the primaries where Kennedy was not initially a favorite, and the first primary where Kennedy's Catholicism would be fairly tested. Kennedy had run in the West Virginia primary against his father's advice,* and knew that he had to win it to stay alive. He was back in Washington on primary night, after a completely financed and flawlessly organized campaign, whose only minus moment had come when Franklin Roosevelt, Jr., campaigning for Kennedy in the mountain "hollers" where every shack had a picture of FDR on the wall, had cast tasteless aspersions on Hubert Humphrey's World War II record.

---

* Once, vacationing with the Kennedys at Ambassador Joseph P. Kennedy's fancy house in Palm Beach, Fla., Tony and I had been allowed to sit in on an informal skull session about primary strategy. When the question of West Virginia came up for discussion, Joe Kennedy argued strenuously against JFK's entering: "It's a nothing state and they'll kill him over the Catholic thing." A few minutes later JFK spoke out: "Well, we've heard from the ambassador, and we're all very grateful, Dad, but I've got to run in West Virginia."

The Kennedys asked us to sweat the vote out with them at dinner, but dinner was over long before any remotely meaningful results were in. After a quick call to brother Bobby at the Kanawha Hotel in Charleston we all got into Kennedy's car and drove to the Trans-Lux theater to see *Suddenly Last Summer*. Bad omen. It was a film with a surprise ending, whose publicity included a warning that no one would be admitted after the show had started. And no one included the next president of the United States. No manner of identification could change the usher's instructions, and so we walked catty-corner across New York Avenue and Fourteenth Street to the Plaza theater, which, then as now, specialized in porn. This wasn't the hard-core porn of the seventies, just a nasty little thing called *Private Property* starring one Katie Manx as a horny housewife who kept getting raped and seduced by hoodlums. We wondered aloud if the movie was on the Catholic index of forbidden films (it was), and whether or not there were any votes in it either way for Kennedy in allegedly anti-Catholic West Virginia if it were known that he was in attendance. Kennedy's concentration was absolute zero; he left every twenty minutes to call Bobby in West Virginia. Each time he returned, he'd whisper "Nothing definite yet," slouch back into his seat and flick his teeth with the fingernail of the middle finger on his right hand until he left to call again.

When we got back to their house on N Street, the telephone was ringing. It was Bobby and it was victory —big. Modest war whoops were let fly, a bottle of champagne we had brought—in case—was opened, and the *Caroline* was ordered up for the flight to West Virginia and a post-midnight victory appearance. Would Tony and I like to go along? Would we ever! Or at least would I ever; Tony didn't like flying, and the Charleston airport had unfortunately been referred to that night as challenging. But I knew it was the political story of the week, and I knew that the whole night, plus the flight down, would give me the personal detail and color that editors of newsmagazines crave (and dine out on). Tony got more than she bargained for with a trip so bumpy that Jean Smith screamed for her husband Steve all the way down. I got exactly what I bargained for, especially in Hugh Sidey's expression, as my opposite number on *Time* watched me get off the plane at the Charleston airport behind the candidate.

Once in West Virginia for the victory appearance, Kennedy ignored Jackie, and she seemed miserable at being left out of things. She was then far from the national figure she later became in her own right. And this night, she and Tony stood on a stairway, totally ignored, as JFK made his victory statement on television. Later, when Kennedy was enjoying his greatest moment of triumph to date, with everyone in the hall shouting and yelling, Jackie quietly disappeared and went out to the car and sat by herself until he was ready to fly back to Washington.

The first trip we ever took with the Kennedys had been on a small chartered airplane from Annapolis to Hyannisport in September, 1959. We first drove to one of those mindless regional political throws that JFK attended regularly as an unannounced presidential candidate. This one was in Prince George's County, Maryland, in one of those motel convention halls that became a home away from home for Kennedy during the next year. I remember most watching Jackie, and the almost physical discomfort she showed as she walked slowly into this crowded hall to get stared at

—not talked to, just simply stared at. Her reaction, later to become so familiar, was simply to pull some invisible shade down across her face and cut out spiritually. She was physically present, but intellectually long gone. We were to see that expression a hundred times in the years to come. Later on the bumpy plane ride to the Cape she and Tony talked about how they hated such functions, how difficult they found it to plug into random conversations, how impossible it was to have a meaningful conversation with anyone under those circumstances. They never changed, unable to treat these things like trips to the zoo, where the animals stare at you because they aren't free to do anything else, and where you can stare at that particularly interesting animal, 'the American voter, as he changes his spots from one corner of the country to the other.

When we got to the Kennedy compound in Hyannisport, long after midnight, Kennedy walked without a word to the kitchen, opened the icebox, and pulled out a huge tureen of clam chowder. Apparently the cook was under instructions to have an endless supply on hand in case His Nibs wanted a snack. We watched in fascination as he gulped down four large bowls, one after the other. In anyone else it would have been gluttonous.

We played golf, went for a picnic cruise in the ambassador's motor yacht, walked on the beach, and swam. Someone took a picture of JFK and me in our bathing suits, on a sailfish, the small boat that consists only of a plank and a mast. When he saw the photograph the next day, he was horrified. "It shows the Fitzgerald breasts," he said, as he handed it to the rest of us, and in fact it did show the future president

"We played golf, went for a picnic cruise in the ambassador's motor yacht, walked on the beach, and swam. Someone took a picture of JFK and me in our bathing suits, on a sailfish, the small boat that consists only of a plank and a mast. When he saw the photograph the next day, he was horrified. 'It shows the Fitzgerald breasts,' he said, as he handed it to the rest of us, and in fact it did show the future president with some extra mammary protuberance. 'Better get rid of that,' he said."

with some extra mammary protuberance. "Better get rid of that," he said.

A few months after the victory in West Virginia, I flew to Los Angeles the week before the Democratic National Convention, and a week before Kennedy arrived, to help write the convention cover story for *Newsweek*. If it's a close race, that pre-convention issue is the toughest news magazine assignment there is. The cover must be picked the Wednesday before the convention starts, exactly five days before the candidate will be selected. The story must be finished late Saturday afternoon, two days before the face on the cover will either be the nominee—and make the magazine's editors look omniscient—or just another losing candidate—and make the magazine's political reporters look for work. *Newsweek* had decided to put its chips on Kennedy (*Time* came out the following Monday with Lyndon B. Johnson on the cover, and if I live to be a hundred I'll never forget the worried and insecure looks on the faces of the *Newsweek* editors as they scanned the opposition), but despite the assurances of the Kennedy insiders who were lassoing and counting delegates, especially the greatest counter of them all, Larry O'Brien, I wasn't sure, and was still looking for every bit of inside information I could find. Tony had arranged to fly out on the same commercial plane with Kennedy early Sunday morning, and Saturday night I telephoned her with a list of last-minute questions for him. She wrote them down on a piece of paper, and when she sat next to him for a time on the plane next day, gave him my list. He was having throat problems, and to save his voice, he took the list and wrote in his answers. Unfortunately that piece of paper didn't survive the convention week, and now

I can only remember one question and answer for sure. It was the first question: "What about Lyndon Johnson for vice-president?" and his tantalizing answer: "He'll never take it."

The convention itself is pretty much a blur to me now, remembered mostly for a fear I can still feel that I had been wrong in urging *Newsweek* to run Kennedy on the cover, and by bits and pieces of evidence, such as they were, that I might in fact be wrong. Notable in that latter category were the standing ovation given Mrs. Eleanor Roosevelt as she entered the convention hall, and the fantastic demonstration staged on the convention floor on behalf of Adlai E. Stevenson. Halfway through the Stevenson demonstration I figured that I'd blown it through naivete and inexperience (this was my first political convention) and that I was going into the history books—the wrong way. I kept looking for comfort to Ken Crawford, my bureau chief and the best working journalist I've ever run across. "Just look at the delegates, Bradlee," he kept saying. "They're not demonstrating." And, by God, they weren't. At first glance it looked as if everyone on the floor was screaming and waving something. But a careful look showed most of the delegates sitting quietly, half-hidden by demonstrators.

The same agonizing wait recurred four months later —this time in the Hyannis National Guard armory waiting through election night and well into the next day for the final verdict of the voters. Journalistically that week was easy; whoever won, the magazine's schedule was such that the choice of the next cover and my next assignment would be automatic. But however much I had tried to be fair and objective in my reporting of the campaign, I now wanted Kennedy to win. I wanted my friend and neighbor to be president. It wasn't that I didn't like Richard Nixon. I had covered him for several weeks during the campaign, and I just didn't know him. I never got close to understanding him. I never got behind that stagy, programmed exterior to anything like an inner man that I could understand, or laugh with.*

It seemed to me then, as it seems to me now, that where Kennedy was instinctively graceful and natural, Nixon was instinctively graceless and programmed. Anyway, I wanted Kennedy to win. When Illinois finally put him over the top, Tony and I walked back to the Yachtsman Motel to find a message asking us to come over to the Kennedys' for supper at their house with Bill Walton, the ex-journalist, artist, Kennedy worker, and Kennedy friend. We arrived early, Tony great with child, and were greeted by Jackie in the same condition. When Kennedy came downstairs, be-

---

* Two years later I covered Nixon again when he was running for governor of California against Pat Brown. Once during that campaign I was driving with Brown between campaign stops when he turned around from the front seat where he was sitting next to his driver and asked me: "Tell me, why do all you guys from the eastern newspapers always refer to Pat Brown as a bumbling horse's ass?" It endeared Governor Brown to me and I couldn't help reflecting that Nixon's inability to ask a similarly self-deprecating question was part of his problem with the press.

At the end of that campaign, after Nixon gave his "farewell" press conference after being beaten by Brown, Kennedy said he thought Richard Nixon was "mentally unsound" or, as he once said of him, "sick, sick, sick." "Nobody could talk like that and be normal," Kennedy said, referring to the famous remark that "You won't have Nixon to kick around anymore." Before the 1960 Kennedy-Nixon debates, JFK didn't really dislike Nixon, much to the annoyance of many of his card-carrying anti-Nixon friends. But during the 1960 campaign he came to dislike the vice-president, and once said to me, "Anyone who can't beat Nixon doesn't deserve to be president."

fore any of us could say a word, he flashed that smile and said to the women: "Okay, girls, you can take out the pillows now. We won."

Over cocktails we nervously asked what we should call him; "Mr. President" sounded awfully awesome, and he was not yet president, yet "Jack" was yesterday. He allowed modestly as how "Prez" would be just fine for now. (Later, when he was in fact president, we called him "Jack" only when we were alone with him or with his close friends, and "Mr. President" whenever anyone else was present.) Over dinner, he told how he had called Chicago's Mayor Richard Daley while Illinois was hanging in the balance to ask how he was doing. "Mr. President," Kennedy quoted Daley as saying, "with a little bit of luck and the help of a few close friends, you're going to carry Illinois." Later, when Nixon was being urged to contest the 1960 election, I often wondered about that statement. I was told—by a member of the task force established by Nixon to decide whether or not to contest it—that the Republicans could well have stolen as many votes in southern Illinois as Daley might have stolen in Cook County.

After dinner, in a relaxed and mischievous mood, Kennedy turned to Walton and me and said, "Okay, I'll give each one of you guys one appointment, one job to fill. What will it be?" Walton spoke up first and told Kennedy he should replace J. Edgar Hoover, by then head of the FBI for more than thirty-six years. I had been growingly concerned about the lack of responsible oversight of the CIA, based on my experience as a foreign correspondent, and so my suggested appointment was a new CIA head to replace Allen Dulles, who had run the agency since 1953 and was the "godfather" of the American intelligence community.

Next morning, I was back in the Kennedy compound in Hyannisport to start work on *Newsweek*'s next cover story, "Robert F. Kennedy . . . The New Man to See in Washington." I was waiting in a small room in Bob Kennedy's house, only to learn that in the next room John Kennedy was meeting with his most intimate advisors, already at work on the transition period. Suddenly, John Kennedy's friend and campaign worker, Lem Billings, came out in the hall. I heard him pick up the phone and say: "Operator, the president-elect would like to place two calls urgently. One to Mr. J. Edgar Hoover at the FBI and one to Mr. Allen Dulles at the CIA." The next voice I heard was Kennedy's, and he was telling J. Edgar Hoover how much he wanted him, was counting on him, to stay on during the Kennedy administration. Laid it on a bit thick, I thought. A few minutes later, the whole scene was repeated with Allen Dulles. Thus ended my career as a presidential consultant. Kennedy's offer and Walton's and my suggestions were made in jest, of course, but I never once recommended anyone to Kennedy after that, in or out of jest.

Only once was I asked to recommend someone to Kennedy for a job. The request came from James Angleton, a friend who held a top position in the Dirty Tricks department of the CIA and who was fired from the agency years later, during the fuss about CIA involvement in domestic intelligence. He called me—from a telephone booth, as is Jim's wont—to arrange lunch with all the trimmings at the Rive Gauche restaurant, then one of the favorite hangouts of CIA executives. The man he was recommending—I could hardly believe my ears—was Cord Meyer, Jr., an old friend, once married to my sister-in-law,* and the job he urged me to propose to Kennedy for Cord was ambassador to Guatemala. The request was extraordinary for three reasons: first, this was only months after the Bay of Pigs fiasco, where the CIA had led Kennedy down the garden path to disaster, and Guatemala was one of the countries where the CIA had trained anti-Castro Cubans for their deaths; second, although I had long known Meyer, and admired him enormously when he was working for the American Veterans' Committee and for World Federalism after returning much decorated from the war, our relations had become strained as a result of my decision to be a journalist and his derisive scorn of the people's right to know; and finally, Kennedy did not like Meyer. Apparently when Meyer was Harold Stassen's aide at the San Francisco U.N. organizing conference in 1945, Kennedy had tried to interview Meyer—unsuccessfully. He, too, had fallen victim, but permanantly, to the philosophy of "Don't get mad; get even." I never relayed Angleton's suggestion.

Another vivid memory involves my son Dino, then about to be two. It was Thanksgiving Day, 1960, and Tony and Jackie were in different hospitals having Marina Bradlee† and John Kennedy, Jr. Kennedy had

---

* Mary Meyer was my wife's sister, and Cord Meyer's ex-wife. She was murdered, while walking on the towpath of the C & O Canal in Georgetown, in October, 1964.

† For some months before Marina was born we had been asking Kennedy if he were in a political and religious position to be the godfather of the child of technically Episcopalian, but actually unaffiliated, parents. This was before Pope John XXIII made ecumenism a household word, but Kennedy was intrigued. It never happened, and Marina was never christened, but every Christmas until his death Christmas presents would arrive from the White House, inscribed "To Marina from her Godfather, John F. Kennedy."

been elected a few weeks earlier, but not yet inaugurated. N Street in Georgetown was a mess, cordoned off for sightseers and the reporters who kept a permanent watch from various neighborhood houses. And Kennedy asked me if I would like to bring Dino and join him and Caroline for a drive to Virginia and tea with his mother-in-law, Mrs. Hugh D. Auchincloss. I would—despite Dino's appearance. The day before, Dino had taken a swan dive from the top rung of the jungle gym onto the cement of Hyde playground, ending up in the emergency room of Georgetown Hospital for stitches on his forehead. The only coat I could find for him on this cold autumn day was the coat in which he had swanned, covered with blood. I didn't give it much thought as we walked the few feet from our house to his, until the reporters and TV cameramen suddenly surged toward us—toward Dino, really, seeing a pretty good "photographic opportunity" for a slow holiday in the president-elect and his immaculately dressed daughter tooling off in a Secret Service limousine with me and my bloody, grubby, motherless child. Kennedy relished the prospect of a meeting between Dino, looking the way he did, and the formal Mrs. Auchincloss at a formal tea in the formal halls of Merrywood. During the twenty-minute ride, Dino must have crawled between the front and back seats at least twenty times, his feet and hands striking out blindly, and Kennedy couldn't take his eyes off him. "Well, I suppose if you could have only one thing," he said, "it would be that—energy. Without it, you haven't got a thing."

A few days before Thanksgiving, the Kennedys had helped us out of a serious jam, involving the birth of Marina, with the world's most highly qualified babysitter. Tony had had five previous children with exactly thirty minutes' warning each. I had carefully practiced the drive from N Street to the Washington Hospital Center, and had it down to a tough twenty minutes. When the magic moment came at 10:00 P.M. the night of November 23, I had ten minutes to spare—and no sitter. We had a Dutch girl living in with us that year, but she was in night school and never got home before midnight. In desperation I called Jackie and asked if her maid, Provie (Providencia Paredes), whom the children knew, might be available. Provie had left for parts unknown a few minutes before. I was just about to abandon the children, when the president-elect called to ask if it were really an emergency. "You're goddamn right, it's an emergency," I said. "I've got about a minute and a half right now, if I'm lucky." Kennedy said that maybe he could send one of his Secret Service agents around to watch the kids, and I could only mutter "Please," weakly, before I had to hang up and rush to the hospital. We made it with only a minute or so to spare, and when I got home long after midnight, there was Andy, age ten, sitting totally absorbed on the floor, watching a Secret Service agent* take his .45 caliber pistol apart and put it together again for the umpteenth time. It was the only time to my knowledge that I accepted free service from the United States government—at least until I rode free in a helicopter in Vietnam.

Sidewalk press conferences by the president-elect on the stoop in front of his house were common occurrences in the cold of November and December, 1960. Reporters damn near froze on the street between these conferences, and occasionally men like Al Otten of

---

* It is against the policy of the Secret Service to identify this agent, whose name I lost in the confusion of the moment. I thank him now, anonymously and belatedly.

the *Wall Street Journal* and the late Bill Lawrence of the *New York Times* and ABC would drop in on us to use the john or the phone, or partake of spiritual refreshment. Lawrence once ordered up a very dry double martini in the dead of night, and we sent my stepdaughter Nancy Pittman, then age nine, in wrapper and slippers, down with it, telling her to give it to the funny-looking man with the Russian caracul hat.

One sidewalk press conference that made all the history-books but that never in fact occurred involved Kennedy's determination to name his brother attorney general. When I learned it was in the offing, I asked Kennedy how he intended to make the sensitive announcement. "Well," he said,, "I think I'll open the front door of the Georgetown house some morning about 2:00 A.M., look up and down the street, and if there's no one there, I'll whisper 'It's Bobby.' "

Two other incidents on N Street are still vivid in my mind, so many years later. The first occurred on January 24, the first Sunday morning after Kennedy became president. It was about eleven o'clock. Tony was changing diapers, and if the truth will out, I was in the bathroom, when Dino came running upstairs, mumbling something about "president" and "downstairs" and "lot of people." At that time in his young life, just over two years old, we had noticed he was prone to exaggeration, to say the least, and we had often lectured him on the subject. This looked like the time for another lecture, and I was just about to start when I looked out the bathroom window and saw a large crowd. Just at this moment we heard that familiar voice shout upstairs: "Isn't there anybody in this house who is going to greet the president of the United States?" He had not even rung the bell, and I suppose, if we had thought of it at all, we had assumed that any visit to our house by the president would have involved more planning or ceremony.

Kennedy had relished the preparations for the pomp and circumstance of his inauguration, and liked to be teased about the fact that he so obviously did relish it. The perfect tease came from a classic typo in an early edition of the *Boston Globe,* announcing that Richard Cardinal Cushing would deliver the invocation when Kennedy was sworn in as the thirty-fifth president of the United States.

"Richard Cardinal Cushing today accepted the invitation," the *Globe* story read, "to deliver the invocation at the inauguration of Saint John Kennedy as President of the United States." We called him Saint John for a few days after that.

One future visit—the only other time Kennedy ever visited our house—sure as hell did involve planning and ceremony. I had asked the future president a long time earlier for only one favor—that he and Jackie come to dinner one night to meet my father and mother, and they did, a few weeks after they were in the White House. My father was a wonderful, strong, and witty man, but he was a lifelong Republican, as were all Bradlees since my great-great-grandfather and namesake, Benjamin Williams Crowninshield, ran for Congress from Salem, Massachusetts—and lost to my great-great-granduncle, Rufus Choate. The first political anecdote I ever heard in our family concerned my cousin Frank Crowninshield (known as "Bad Frank" to distinguish him from "Good Frank" Crowninshield, the founder and editor of *Vanity Fair* magazine). It seems that in the mid-thirties Bad Frank literally had a pain in the ass of sufficient discomfort to require an X-ray. Just as the machine was lowered into position over his posterior, so the story went endlessly, Bad Frank turned to the X-ray technician and told her: "Make it a good likeness, nurse, so that I can send it to that goddamn fool in the White House."

My father had known Joe Kennedy very slightly, first when the future ambassador to the Court of St. James was coaching the Harvard freshman baseball team, and later when my father was working for thirty-five dollars a month as a secretary to the president of a bank with whom Kennedy senior had business. My father had been fascinated by all my stories about Jack Kennedy, and since he couldn't stand Mr. Nixon, it looked very much as if he were going to throw caution and tradition to the winds and vote for a Democrat —as he did. The day the Kennedys came to dinner, it snowed like hell, and I stayed home from work for a few hours to shovel off a small section of the sidewalk. It didn't seem right somehow to let the president and the first lady slosh through the snow. While I was breaking my back, I noticed three guys across the street, leaning on their shovels, just hanging around watching me. Of course, when I was finished, they moved across and shoveled our sidewalk for thirty feet on either side of the house. They had been sent by Captain Kennedy of Number Seven Precinct, who in turn had been alerted by the Secret Service. Captain Kennedy and Secret Service types arrived a few minutes later, asking for more information than we had about the guests (Harry Labouisse, who was being considered for some job in the Kennedy administration, and his wife, the former Eve Curie; and Walter and Helen Lippmann, old friends of my parents) and the people helping Tony in the kitchen, especially the redoubtable Mary Booten, who had been with us since we returned to Washington from Paris.

I can remember only two things about the dinner.

First, my old man didn't have too many martinis before dinner, which he had been known to have; and Kennedy made us tell the story about how we had been unable for two years to get our daughter, Nancy, accepted into some posh dancing class, despite references that had included Mrs. Borden Harriman, Mrs. Gifford Pinchot, and a host of other acceptables. Kennedy loved that story, because in Boston, he said, people like the Bradlees had kept people like the Kennedys out of many more significant institutions than dancing classes. At the end of the story, he turned to my father and said, "If that had happened to Dad, he would have moved the whole family out of Boston."

In the First Hundred Days, we were seeing the Kennedys occasionally with some regularity, except for the time around the Bay of Pigs disaster, and Kennedy and I would talk occasionally on the telephone. Gone were the regular Saturday morning telephone calls, which he used to make to me in my office before he assumed the presidency, checking on next week's Periscope items, and ready to share gossip if an urgent, last-minute call for better items had come from *Newsweek* in New York, as it so often did Saturday mornings.

When we did talk, Kennedy more often than not was preoccupied with foreign affairs, particularly Laos and Cuba. During his campaign, Kennedy had not stressed foreign affairs for several reasons. First, it was not his particular field of expertise, and Nixon was claiming foreign affairs as his own best bailiwick. Second, there were not all that many foreign policy issues kicking around. Quemoy and Matsu was perhaps the major foreign policy problem. Planning for the invasion of Cuba was well under way, but Kennedy didn't learn about it until after he was elected, and Nixon couldn't bring it up during the campaign. But after Kennedy had been in office four months, forces pushed his nose into foreign policy issues, particularly that mixture of foreign policy and military issues that ultimately forced Lyndon Johnson to leave the White House.

"In the entire first (FDR) Roosevelt campaign," the president told me at this time, "foreign affairs were mentioned only once, and then in one paragraph of one speech on the last day of the campaign." But on the anniversary of the first First Hundred Days, Kennedy expressed concern about the national capacity to solve problems like Laos and Cuba, which he had not defined in his campaign. "We can prevent one nation's army from moving across the border of another nation," he said. "We are strong enough for that. And we are probably strong enough to prevent one nation from unleashing nuclear weapons on another. But we can't prevent infiltration, assassination, sabotage, bribery, any of the weapons of guerrilla warfare." Kennedy said he had learned a new, and discouraging, math: "One guerrilla can pin down twelve conventional soldiers, and we've got nothing equivalent." He spoke to me several times of "the six or seven thousand guerrillas" poised in North Vietnam, ready, willing, and able to present him with his next foreign crisis.

The Bay of Pigs shook his confidence—almost beyond repair—in the CIA and in the Joint Chiefs of Staff. Right after the fiasco, and after he had quickly accepted responsibility, he was philosophical. "Presumably," he said, "I was going to learn these lessons some time, and maybe better sooner, than later."

Cuba taught him something else, which was probably more significant in the long run: that elevation to this high office inhibited the free-flowing informality between President Kennedy and his associates in a way that it never did between Senator Kennedy and his associates. He made this point one night by telling how he once asked Dave Powers during the campaign in some jerkwater hotel to hand him his shoes. "Get them yourself, damn it," the president quoted Powers as replying. "You're not my commander-in-chief yet." Jackie weighed in with another story about "Mugsy" O'Leary, another *Last Hurrah* type from Boston, who cut a considerable swath through Georgetown as the Kennedys' chauffeur. Jackie said she had been dawdling around one day, late for an appointment to meet her husband somewhere, when Mugsy had shouted to her: "Come on, Jackie, for Chrissake move your ass." Old "Mugs" wouldn't be putting it so bluntly now, we all agreed.

"John's Other Wife—Part One"

(This first contemporaneously written record of a conversation with President Kennedy seems strangely trivial so long after the fact. The fact that it was the first conversation I recorded at the time is significant to me now. I obviously felt that the story might not be trivial, and that as a journalist, I had to make special efforts to explore potentially harmful information which I could well ignore as a friend.

As a friend, it would have made no difference to me if Kennedy had been married umpteen times before he married Jacqueline Bouvier. But as a journalist, a previous Kennedy marriage would have been so inconsistent with the existing Kennedy image that it would have been historically and politically significant.)

AUGUST 14, 1961 / Historically, this was a week of crisis over Berlin. Six days later, on August 20, the president ordered 1,500 U.S. troops down the autobahn into Berlin.

But inside the White House, it was the week of the Blauvelt crisis—known irreverently to the Washington press corps when the crisis went public as "John's Other Wife"—the week that "documentary" evidence surfaced indicating that John Kennedy had been married secretly and unsuccessfully before he had married Jackie in 1953.

We were gossiping with the Kennedys and the president's college roommate, Congressman Torbert Mac-Donald of Massachusetts, when Pierre Salinger arrived in the middle of dinner. He asked to see the president privately and they left the room for about three minutes. We didn't know it at the time, but Salinger was telling Kennedy for the first time about the surfacing of his "other wife."

I first heard of the case two days later via a telephone call from James Truitt, a former *Time* correspondent who was then working as an assistant to Philip L. Graham, publisher of the *Washington Post*. Truitt's story briefly was that some irate D.A.R. type had walked into the city room of the *Post*, announcing that she had documentary proof of an earlier Kennedy marriage, that she had offered the story to the *Chicago Tribune*, which had refused to print it. Her proof, she told the *Post*, was a privately printed book called *The Blauvelt Family Genealogy*, published in 1957, U.S. Library of Congress catalog card number 56–10936, and readily available in that library. The guts of her evidence was a paragraph listing a Blauvelt descendant by the name of Durie Malcolm, whose third marriage, it was said, was to John F. Kennedy, son of Joseph P. Kennedy. Truitt told me he thought he could get a photostatic copy of the entry, not from the Library of Congress, but from the D.A.R. library. I tried the Library of Congress, only to be told pointedly that the book was out, and that the waiting list included ten members of Congress.

Truitt arrived at my office at 6:00 P.M., with the photostat, and sure enough on page 884, where the eleventh generation of Blauvelts was being treated, in entry number 12,427, lay this nugget: "Durie (Kerr) Malcolm. We have no birthdate. She was born Kerr, but took the name of her stepfather. She first married Firmin Desloge IV. They were divorced. Durie then married F. John Bersbach. They were divorced, and she married, third, John F. Kennedy, son of Joseph P. Kennedy, onetime Ambassador to England. There were no children of the second or third marriages."

It wasn't until August 20 that I got what I believe is the complete story from the president himself, and from other sources that will be obvious from what follows. Salinger said he had received only one query on this subject until Truitt and I called him—a query from an assistant to the right-wing commentator Fulton Lewis. Salinger told us he had learned from other sources that both the *Boston Herald* and the *Chicago Tribune* had been given the contents of the Blauvelt book, but neither had made any inquiries of him. A "friendly" congressman was Salinger's source, and several of his "unfriendly" congressional colleagues—presumably including those on the Library of Congress waiting list—were reportedly licking their chops in anticipation of a scandal.

On Wednesday, August 15, Salinger went looking for Louis Leon Blauvelt, author of the 1,000-page genealogy, only to find that he was dead. He found Blauvelt's son-in-law, one William K. Smith, of East Orange, N.J., the new keeper of the Blauvelt family records. At Salinger's request, Smith examined all the records from which Blauvelt had written the book. Again at Salinger's request, Smith executed an affidavit stating there was no evidence in those records of any such marriage. Smith told Salinger that he had found a yellowed, 1947 clipping from a Miami newspaper, reporting that John F. Kennedy had been seen in a Miami nightclub with Durie Malcolm. Kennedy later confirmed to me that he had dated her once, but that she had been a girl friend of his brother, Joe.

With information provided him by the president, Salinger then went looking for Durie Malcolm. In fact, she had been married for the last fourteen years to Thomas Shevlin, a Palm Beach playboy and onetime husband of Lorraine Cooper, wife of the then senator from Kentucky, John Sherman Cooper. Salinger told me that Durie Malcolm Shevlin had also executed an affidavit, swearing she had never been married to John F. Kennedy. I tried to call Mrs. Shevlin every day for at least a week, and in each case the operator reported that her telephone had been disconnected at "the customer's request." I did contact one Blauvelt relative, who insisted on being unidentified, trying to find out if Blauvelt was in fact wrong, how come he was wrong. The relative said, "It was just one colossal mistake, that's all." Blauvelt was a "Spaniard," a Spanish-American War veteran, he said, who had spent more than thirty years researching his family, and "may well have concluded that the family hadn't done much and likely just formed the idea in his mind. That's all."

This relative said he had noticed the Malcolm-Kennedy entry when the book came out, but said nothing about it since "I knew it was wrong." He didn't say how he knew it was wrong. And he told me the *New York Daily News* had contacted him two months previously.

Before I talked to Kennedy about his "other wife," I had briefed Oz Elliott, the editor of *Newsweek,* and he had a St. Louis stringer do some digging on Bersbach. According to St. Louis court records, Durie Malcolm divorced Bersbach in the summer of 1938 and resumed her maiden name. On January 3, 1939, the St. Louis papers ran an account of her marriage to Desloge. On January 24, 1947, they were divorced in St. Louis County Court, Clayton, Mo. And on January 21, 1948, they sued each other for custody of their one child. She claimed in her suit that Desloge had failed to return the child after a Christmas visit. He counterclaimed that she was off on a safari—with Shevlin. On July 12, 1947, she and Shevlin were married before a justice of the peace at Fort Lee, N.J.

This research produced the first discrepancies in Blauvelt's account. In his book, he had Durie Malcolm marrying Desloge first, then Bersbach. In fact, she married Bersbach first and Desloge second. Also, although the book was not published until 1957, it made no mention of the marriage of Malcolm and Shevlin in 1947.

Analytically, records show that this woman was unmarried—and thus technically in a position to marry Kennedy—twice. Once between the summer of 1938 and January, 1939, when Kennedy was a junior at Harvard. And once between January and July of 1947, the first six months of Kennedy's first term in Congress.

One of the penalties of being a reporter and a

friend of someone in high office is that the reporter is regularly called upon—in conscience and in response to the editors unburdened by such friendship—to explore potentially derogatory information about his friend with even greater zeal than would be devoted to similar information about a non-friend. The general public doesn't believe this, nor did all of President Nixon's men many years later, but it is true.

And so when I finally talked to Kennedy about Durie Malcolm, I think I had more information about the alleged scandal than any other reporter. I was ready . . . and he was amused. The first thing he told me was, "You have met her." This I could not believe but he went on: "You remember one day we played golf at Seminole (in Palm Beach), and we went into the pro shop and there was this girl on the sofa and a guy standing next to her? Well, that was Durie Malcolm and that was Shevlin." And I did remember. It was three in the afternoon, and the girl was lying on the sofa, her feet over the arm rest. Everybody was tanned as leather and they looked to me as though they might have had too many cocktails at lunch. "She was a girl friend of my brother Joe," he went on, "and I took her out a couple of times, I guess. That's all."

And then suddenly: "You haven't got it, Benjy. You're all looking to tag me with some girl, and none of you can do it, because it just isn't there." Jackie just listened with a smile on her face. And that is the closest I ever came to hearing him discuss his reputation as what my father used to call "a fearful girler."

"Is it too late to change covers?"

FEBRUARY 9, 1962 / This was the third of the White House dances, like the rest a dazzling mixture of "beautiful people" from New York, jet-setters from Europe, politicians, reporters (always reporters) who are friends, and Kennedy relatives. The crowd is always young. The women are always gorgeous, and you have to pinch yourself to realize that you are in the Green Room of the White House and that fellow who just fell on the dance floor with Helen Chavchavadze is no stag line bum but the vice-president of the United States, Lyndon Baines Johnson.

We first dined at Bill Walton's in Georgetown, part of the group that tried to convince itself that we were so out (in not getting an invitation to dinner at the White House) that we were in. The Kennedys couldn't afford to snub anyone that way except their really good friends, we told each other edgily.

It was also the night of the release of Gary Powers, the pilot of the U-2 reconnaissance plane shot down over central Russia in May of 1960. He had been convicted of espionage by a Soviet military tribunal, sentenced to ten years' "deprivation of freedom," and Kennedy had been trying for months to get him out of jail through an exchange for some Soviet spy in our custody.

At about 11:30 P.M., Kennedy came across the dance floor to tell me he had a helluva story for me and to ask me if it was too late to change the cover

49

on the magazine. (It *was* too late; the cover stayed on Vietnam and guerrilla warfare.) If nothing else, his question indicated that it was a big story, for I had come to trust his judgment on cover stories (as well as his knowledge of what covers were running in up-coming magazines. Several times, when the editors of *Newsweek* felt they really had to know what *Time* had on its upcoming cover, I was able to get the answer from the president, and he was never wrong.), and I tried for fifteen minutes to get the story out of him, without success. I had been talking to his sister, Jean Smith, and he drew her aside to whisper the story to her, but I couldn't get it out of her, either. As we left, the president told me to meet him under the Franklin portrait—in the Green Room—at 12:30 A.M.

I was there promptly, talking to Kay Graham, wife of the publisher of the *Washington Post,* when he took me aside and gave me the word: Powers had been swapped for Colonel Rudolph Abel, a colonel in the Soviet intelligence agency, and the highest-ranking Communist spy ever caught in the U.S., who had been fingered by a defector and convicted of conspiring to collect military secrets. The story would be announced in a couple of hours. Again, he asked if it was too late for *Newsweek* to change covers.

If it was too late for *Newsweek,* it was perhaps not too late for our sister publication, the *Washington Post,* and I went looking for Phil Graham to ask him if the *Post* still had an edition available. It did, and Phil pulled me over to a telephone, sitting on the sill of a large window in the main hall of the White House, and put in a call to Richard Thornburgh, the *Post*'s night managing editor. After a few seconds of conversation, Graham handed me the phone and said, "Okay, buster, start dictating." It was another one of those experiences that are hard to comprehend, even now. Imagine a reporter dictating an exclusive story from the best of all possible sources to the strains of a dance orchestra playing inside the White House! It was the kind of thing that made Kennedy nervous about me, and the kind of thing that made me nervous about the personal relationship, but not nervous enough to sacrifice the professional challenge and thrill.

The *Post* caught 165,000 copies of the home-delivered edition with my story, leading the paper with it, and had a world beat for two hours, much to the discomfort of Salinger, who was going to brief the press with his own exclusive. When Graham and I rejoined the party, the other reporters present (Tom Ross of the *Chicago Sun-Times*, Bill Lawrence of ABC, and Rowland Evans, the columnist) were edgy and sure something was up. Kennedy had kept disappearing, and now Graham and I had split, but they stayed in the dark until Salinger hauled them away for his 3:00 A.M. briefing. At 2:00 A.M., Kennedy had disappeared again, this time, he told me later, to an open line with Berlin and assurance that the prisoner exchange had been consummated. When he got that word, he flashed a go-ahead sign to Salinger, rejoined the party, and stayed there until 4:30 in the morning. By that time, Tony and I both agreed that he seemed a bit high—one of the very rare occasions we'd seen him in that condition.

In all the time that we knew him, we saw Kennedy really tight only once. The occasion was a small dinner in the family dining room upstairs, with only the president, Lee Radziwill, Bill Walton, and ourselves present. Jackie was out of town. The "twist" had just hit Washington, or at least it had finally hit Washington, and after dinner Lee Radziwill put Chubby Checker's records on and gave all the men lessons. The champagne was flowing like the Potomac in flood and the president himself was opening bottle after bottle in a manner that sent the foam flying over the furniture, shouting "Look at Bill go" to Walton, or "Look at Benjy go" to me, as we practiced with the "princess."

Normally he sipped at a scotch and water without ice, rarely finishing two before dinner, sipped at a glass of wine during dinner, rarely had a drink after dinner, and almost never had a drink in the middle of the day.

"Hard-boiled . . . but, or soft-boiled . . . if"

FEBRUARY 10, 1962 / The president called from Glen Ora (the house they were renting outside of Middleburg), with nothing obviously on his mind. We talked for almost half an hour—about the Powers-Abel swap, about the Charles J. V. Murphy article in *Life*,* and "what a bastard Murphy was," about the hard-boiled, soft-boiled controversy about nuclear testing, and about the party the night before. These conversations without a specific reason or question are fascinating. It's almost

---

* Murphy, an editor of *Fortune* who was a bright star in Henry Luce's conglomerate firmament, had written about the question of to resume or not to resume nuclear testing, had come out plainly for resumption and claimed that Kennedy had fallen into a trap by proposing "one last effort" at bringing off a nuclear treaty with the Soviet Union in the closing days of his presidential campaign.

as if he were lonely, or at least at loose ends, and wanted to crack a few gags and relax, to reach out and touch a friend.

The trouble with the hard-boiled/soft-boiled problem (to resume nuclear testing or to continue the moratorium on nuclear testing), he said, was that so many of the people involved were "hard-boiled . . . but, or soft-boiled . . . if." Some were soft-boiled on one issue and hard-boiled on another. He mentioned Walt Rostow (then head of the State Department's Policy Planning Council, and later President Johnson's advisor for national security affairs) in this connection as one of the more vociferous members of the hard-boiled school where Vietnam is concerned, and—at least by reputation—substantially less so in other areas of the world. On the subject of resumption of nuclear tests, he says that he has not finally decided, but gives the impression that he has, most reluctantly, and that the only issue unresolved is not whether, but when to resume testing. When I mentioned the March 5 plenum session in Moscow and the March 15 disarmament conference as dates before which it was all but impossible politically to resume testing, he seemed relieved that at least he would not have to order a resumption of testing before then.

On the subject of the dance, he rated it the best of the three to date, and solicited suggestions for an occasion to hold another one fairly soon. He thought Bobby and Ethel might be good guests of honor, when they return from their trip around the Far East. Jackie, he said, felt they perhaps should wait until the spring, and he sounded disappointed.

The conversation ended, as these conversations often ended, with his views on some of the women present

—the overall appeal of the daughter of Prince Paul of Yugoslavia and Mary Meyer. "Mary would be rough to live with," Kennedy noted, not for the first time. And I agreed, not for the first time.

"The Jackie Kennedy Show"

FEBRUARY 14, 1962 / We watched "The Jackie Kennedy Show" after dinner at the White House, a one-hour CBS special, produced at a cost of $255,990 and watched by an estimated 46,000,000 people. Jackie used a script only when describing some very old prints, as she strolled from one room to another, describing gifts and remembering donors. "Television at its best," said the *Chicago Daily News*. "A remarkable job," said the show's host, Charles Collingwood. The only other guests at dinner were Max Freedman, the distinguished American correspondent of the *Manchester Guardian,* who had been caught by bad weather in New York and made dinner only after a $100 cab ride from LaGuardia airport, and Mrs. John Randolph ("Fifi") Fell, a New York and Long Island hostess. Jackie had brought Caroline to our house to play with our children that afternoon . . . nurse Maud Shaw's day off.

At cocktails the president was in a garrulous and acerbic mood, rehashing the dance again. He was particularly irritated at a man called Watson Blair, a New York businessman, who had glowered from the dance floor sidelines all night, telling everyone he was having a miserable time. Fifi Fell asked if she could bring Blair any message, and the president said, "Damn right. Tell him he's on the list and not to worry: he won't be asked again." Peter Duchin, jet-set bandleader, son of pianist Eddy Duchin, also made the list for behavior the president considered less than acceptable. He, too, had apparently been critical of something. But there was much upbeat reminiscing, too—Phil Graham's "twist," which had produced a six-inch rip in the seat of his pants as he took his first lesson in the new dance craze from Tony . . . the very proper "twists" performed by Jackie with "the Guv" (Averell Harriman) and Bob McNamara . . . the stable of pretty women from New York, and of course the drama involved in the Powers-Abel swap.

The president couldn't resist bringing up the *Post*'s exclusive with that understatement that was so typical of his humor. Over cocktails he turned to me out of the blue and said, "By the way, who do you work for, anyway?" I wasn't about to admit anything, and it developed that I didn't have to. "Are you making any charges?" I asked. "No," he smiled. "Do you have any statement that you want to make?" And I said simply, "Not at this time," not knowing how sore he was, if in fact he was sore at all. He then said he was about to order an investigation of that leak, but thought it over for twenty-four hours and came to the conclusion that he didn't have to.

"Plucky* gets such a kick out of tracing these leaks back to me," the president said. "I have to be more

---

* Pierre Salinger, Kennedy's press secretary, came to be widely known as "Plucky Pierre," after he was asked at a press briefing if he was going to go on one of those 50-mile hikes, which the Kennedy macho had popularized at the time. Salinger's answer: "I may be plucky, but I'm not stupid."

careful." I then asked him if he was referring to the leak on the Cuban embargo. He smiled and said, "That's one of them." The president later told me he had blown his stack about the premature release of that story and ordered Salinger to spare no effort in finding out who leaked it. Salinger worked like the investigative reporter he used to be for two days, and finally reported back to the president that he was pleased to be able to announce he had traced the leak. "Who was it?" the president asked, eagerly. "You," said Salinger, gleefully. "What do you mean?" Kennedy asked, crestfallen. "Didn't you tell George Smathers (a senator from Florida and an old Kennedy pal in their bachelor days)?" Salinger asked. Kennedy nodded. "Well, George told a friend of his on the *Tampa Tribune* and that was that," Salinger said.

The gifts that King Ibn Saud of Saudi Arabia had left the Kennedys that afternoon were piled on a table in the yellow Oval Room upstairs: a couple of suitcases full of some kind of filmy flowered material, and some clothes. The clothes were hard to believe: a small jacket for young John, the kind that sells for four bucks at Sears, and some pullover jackets that appeared to be made of thin camel hair . . . all of them inside out, apparently to prove that they had never been worn before. The president obviously felt that the relief map of the United States he had given Ibn Saud was a substantially better gift.

After dinner we moved into a small sitting room next to the Lincoln Room to watch Jackie on the show that had been taped a month earlier. There had been a lot of talk at dinner about how good CBS was, what a good director they had in Frank Schaffner, but ironically the president's TV set wouldn't bring in the

CECIL STOUGHTON PHOTO

" 'What makes journalism so fascinating.' President Kennedy once said to me, 'and biography so interesting [is] the struggle to answer that single question: What's he like?'

"He genuinely liked reporters. Once, though, the president blew his stack over a premature news leak about the Cuban embargo. He ordered Salinger to find out who was responsible. Salinger worked like hell for two days, finally reporting back to the president that he was pleased to be able to announce that he had traced the leak. 'Who was it?' asked the president. 'You,' said Salinger gleefully. 'What do you mean?' asked the president. 'Didn't you tell George Smathers?' Salinger asked. 'Well, George told some friend on the Tampa Tribune, and that was that.' "

CBS channel, and we watched the show on NBC, and we watched it in virtual silence. We were all impressed with Jackie's knowledge and poise. She had really thrown herself into the refurbishing of the White House with an energy and ability that had never been used before.* There was one snicker when Collingwood broke off some bromide about how important the past was for the future. And there was movement in the small crowd when the president himself appeared—in what could at best be called a minor role. He was obviously not particularly pleased with that role or his performance in it, and Tony went so far as to say later that she felt the president was actually jealous of Jackie's performance and the attention she got as a result. As soon as the broadcast was over, the telephone started ringing, with Tony answering. (This was quite common at the Kennedy White House—to have guests answer the phone.) One call was from Charlie Bartlett, a newspaper columnist, who was one of Kennedy's oldest friends, and the man who had introduced him to Jackie. The president quoted him as saying that he had "cried during the whole performance," and went on to say, "Yeah, and I cried too, over my performance." Another call was from his sister, Eunice Shriver, who first talked to Kennedy and then asked to speak to Jackie. But Jackie shook her head, and the president said she had gone off to bed—in tears.

We teased Kennedy about calling his wife "Jackie" during the CBS special, the first time to my knowledge

---

* My father had combined his new admiration for the Kennedys with his old love of antiques and had offered the White House a beautiful sideboard desk built in the early nineteenth century for Daniel Webster, with his initials "D.W." carved on the inside. The Kennedys accepted it, and it was used as the private dining room sideboard throughout the Kennedy, Johnson—and Nixon—administrations, and still is as of this writing.

he had ever done so in public, and in that quizzical way of his, almost like a small child looking for approval, he asked us whether we thought "the first lady" would have been more appropriate. (He never spoke of his wife as "Jackie" again in public, as far as I know.)

On the subject of Vietnam, he had this to say: "The trouble is, we are violating the Geneva agreement. Not as much as the North Vietnamese are, but we're violating it. Whatever we have to do, we have to do in some kind of secrecy, and there's a lot of danger in that. The Republicans want it both ways in Vietnam, and that's the privilege of the party not in power. It's like Korea for them. We should have taken the enemy across the Yalu, they used to say, but it was always a Democratic war. Now the Republicans want us to defeat communism in Vietnam by any means, but when we try to do it quietly, they howl that they're not being kept informed and that just means that we are not doing enough. Diem is Diem and the best we've got."

On the subject of Gary Powers, the president did not appear to be up-to-date on how the debriefing of Powers was proceeding, or at least he wasn't telling me. He said he did not know how high Powers was flying when he was hit. (The operating altitude of the U-2s—later revealed to be more than 60,000 feet—was a matter of great speculation at that time). "The questioning is going to take longer than I'd thought," he said. "Up to a month." He showed no inclination to treat Powers either as a hero or as a pariah, but, predictably, he was impressed with Powers' courage. "Whatever else you can say about him, and he's apparently a strange man," the president said, "he's got guts." And of course guts are a big plus in the Kennedy book. Kennedy implied that Powers had been moved from a Maryland hideaway for further questioning in some new CIA hideout in Delaware. I told him about the trouble we were having in getting any member of Powers' family to talk, specifically his sister (Mrs. William E. Hileman of Glassmanor, Md., who told us she had some letters written by Powers from his Soviet jail, and even a snapshot or two of him and his cellmate. She had also complained to a *Washington Post* reporter that she had been unable to pierce the CIA security system and get a message to her brother.). I told the president I was convinced Time-Life had Powers sewn up until he had written his memoirs for them. Kennedy said the United States would have "a helluva lot to say" about what Powers wrote for anybody. He said the government owed Powers between $50,000 and $60,000 in back pay, and had no intention of paying it to him unless the government cleared what he said and wrote.

On the question of Pryor (Frederick L. Pryor, an economics student from Michigan, who disappeared into the Soviet sector of Berlin in August, 1961, was released by the Soviets along with Powers, even though he was a prisoner of the German Democratic Republic), Kennedy felt audibly different. "I wouldn't have busted my ass to get him out of jail all by himself," he said.

"Better than defeat"

MARCH 2, 1962 / I called Kennedy at the White House after his speech announcing the resumption of nuclear testing. (Although they were made as much to solicit information on any subject the president was willing to discuss, these congratulatory calls are actions I would not take now. Any information that I might receive no longer seems to me worth the price of appearing to ingratiate.)

After spending all of three seconds thanking me for my call, the president said: "You know what I liked about your magazine last week? After you really busted one off in us about the urban affairs vote (the Kennedy administration tried unsuccessfully to get the Congress to pass legislation which would create a Department of Urban Affairs in the cabinet, and with it a black secretary-designate, Robert C. Weaver), three or four pages later I read the story about the Negro reaction" —how the Negroes interpreted the vote in Congress as a vote against Kennedy's idea of a black in the cabinet, and how the issue was bound to help Kennedy and the Democrats politically in the 1962 by-elections.

"That's better than defeat, I'll tell you that."

"The coral reef . . . building up"

MARCH 3, 1962 / The president called just after noon to gab—mostly about the resumption of nuclear testing, which he had announced in his speech the night before. His mail was running about even this morning, he said, but that seemed to him to be a good sign. It had been running twenty to one against resumption just before his speech. How did he explain the switch? "First, probably because of the fact that we took a long time to arrive at the decision. Despite what Scotty Reston says, the wrong way to have done it would have been to announce it in November."

Explaining the history of his decision, the president said: "November (the announcement in November 1961 that he was proceeding with preparations for a resumption of testing) was a pretty definite commitment. But there was always a chance that if we could make a deal on Berlin, or if the Soviet tests had been unimpressive, we could have called it off. Of course, we got no place on Berlin, and the results of our analysis of the Soviet tests showed they had made considerable progress." The final decision was reached Tuesday, February 27, at a meeting of the National Security Council, he said, though apparently not all NSC members were present. The president said that about ten persons were there, meeting in the Cabinet Room. Kennedy went around the table asking each person for his recommendation. The vote to resume was unanimous, he said, but he did not announce it at that time. First, he returned to his office to deliberate alone, then reached his decision later that afternoon. He called Prime Minister Harold Macmillan, a man he liked and admired, to inform him. Macmillan asked for a one-day delay so that he could inform his own cabinet, and the president quickly agreed.

In trying to pin down the precise moment in which he reached the decision to resume testing (newsmagazine editors go crazy for that kind of precision), I tried to get him to cooperate, but he wasn't buying. "You have to look at November as a decision of a kind," he said. "I was always reluctant, unless the case for resumption was clearly established. If you had asked me in December, backed me against the wall, I would probably have said 'Go ahead and test.' But there was no real need for a decision in November or December. We were going ahead full speed on the preparation, so there was no drive to decide. There was no real straw that broke the camel's back. It was just a question of the coral reef . . . building up." The way the resumption was announced, Kennedy said, was in line with Gaitskell's advice (Hugh Gaitskell was then the leader of the Labour Party opposition in Britain), but it was also in line with earlier advice he had received from his advisors, notably McGeorge Bundy (his national security expert)—advice he said he really didn't need because he felt the same way himself. Gaitskell reinforced the president's own conviction that an announcement in this way—with one final offer to the Soviets—would be very helpful.

I asked Kennedy if he felt every member of the administration was happy about the decision, not just those present at the February 27 meeting. "I suppose if you grabbed Adlai by the nuts, he might object," he said. (Adlai Stevenson was then U.S. ambassador to the United Nations, and a man whose popularity with liberal Democrats Kennedy resented.) Then with instant enthusiasm he asked me why I didn't call Stevenson and find out how he felt about the resumption of testing. "I'd really like to see what he says."

"How about Weisner (Jerome B. Weisner, the president's scientific advisor)?" I asked. "Jerry's all right," Kennedy answered. "He'd probably have to say there was no real excuse for not testing."

Kennedy, characteristically, closed this conversation abruptly after two pungent observations:

On Nelson Rockefeller, then running for a second term as governor of New York: "He's not doing so well, Lou Harris tells me," and the president was obviously not crushed.

On Robert S. McNamara, his secretary of defense: "He's one of the few guys around this town who, when you ask him if he has anything to say and he hasn't, says 'No.' That's rare these days, I'm telling you."

"Who said Freund?"

MARCH 29, 1962 / Kennedy called shortly before 6:00 P.M. to pass the time of day. First I asked him to confirm the unlikeliest rumor—that he planned to fill the Supreme Court vacancy with Eddie McCormack, nephew of the venerable Speaker of the House and Massachusetts attorney general, who had just announced he would run against Teddy Kennedy in the primary for the Senate, billing himself modestly as "one of America's great legal minds." This produced a snort of derision. In the best of times, the Kennedys and the McCormacks treated each other with polite resentment. But the president wasn't ready to talk about the Supreme Court vacancy. First, he wanted to chew me out for *Newsweek*'s coverage the previous week of Jackie's trip to India. "That wasn't one of your better efforts," he started out, critical, this time, not just thin-skinned, "was it? She's really broken her ass on this trip. You know damn well you can always find some broken-down Englishman or some NBC stringer to knock anything. I don't get all this crap about how she should have been rubbing her nose in the grinding poverty of India. When the French invite you to Paris, they don't show you the sewers; they take you to Versailles."

His displeasure exhausted, I edged the subject over to the tax vote, which he had won that afternoon after it had been languishing in the House for more than a year. With the Supreme Court apportionment case (making federal courts potential arbiters in redistricting cases), the steel strike settlement (two weeks after Kennedy had been instrumental in getting negotiations resumed), and now the tax bill, it was the first really good week he'd had in a long time. "I never saw them look sicker," Kennedy responded, referring to Larry O'Brien and his legislative liaison colleagues at a conference the night before in the president's private living quarters. "Charlie Halleck had the votes to recommit the bill and that would have killed it." Recommittal would have meant defeat on the first of the New Frontier's three big bills, and would dim the future of the other two. He described the problems as "tremendous," and the first problem was the GOP discipline. "We didn't get one single Republican vote on the motion to recommit, and only one on the final vote itself. Second, there was nothing in this bill for anybody. Nobody was lobbying *for* the tax bill. The banks and the savings and loans put on a terrific letter-writing campaign. Jim Delaney (congressman from New York) got 800 handwritten letters in three days. And there we were . . . just *pro bono publico* all the way. We weren't doing anybody any favors. We were just taking it out on somebody's ass wherever we turned. We turned the tide by calling in every chit we had. Twisting, promising, cajoling. I made a few calls, but the leadership really did it: Hale Boggs, Carl Albert, Wilbur Mills" and, as a muted afterthought, "John McCormack."

I finally got him back to ask him about the Supreme Court appointment—which he made, in fact, the next day, but he wasn't in a helpful mood. I told him *Newsweek* had had an interview earlier that week with Paul Freund (Harvard law professor, sometime Kennedy advisor, and a highly respected authority on constitutional law), and pointed out the obvious: the magazine would come up roses if he decided in his wisdom to appoint Freund. "Who said Freund?" the president asked immediately. I told him only that we'd heard it was between Freund and Hastie (William Henry Hastie, a black judge of the U.S. Court of Appeals, Third Circuit). The president was not in the mood to cooperate and didn't even indicate when he would announce his decision.

"WASPs go in more for stealing"

·MARCH 31, 1962 / The president called about 4:30 this afternoon, again with nothing obviously on his mind, but with thirty minutes of conversation. The first subject was Byron "Whizzer" White, the All-American running back turned Rhodes Scholar, pro football star, and deputy attorney general, whose appointment to the Supreme Court had been announced the previous day. He asked what I thought of it, and after I told him I didn't know White that well and knew even less about his legal opinions and philosophy, I asked him how come it was White. "He was just the kind of guy I wanted on the Court," Kennedy said. "Freund was the other choice, but it came down to a question of what the Court needed at this time. I just felt that it did not necessarily need another legal scholar at this time in history. What it needed was a man who understood America, what it was about, and where it was going. That's the law, after all. And on top of that Whizzer (pronounced Whizzah) wouldn't be part of the divisive controversy on the Court now. He's led a broad life. He's had wide experience, and he's also an intellectual and his judgment is good." The president said he knew Freund, had worked closely with him and respected him a great deal.

Again, I tried to get the president to pinpoint the exact timing of his decision on White. He said they had asked Bernard Segal (chairman of the American Bar Association committee which evaluates nominees

67

for federal judgeships) informally about White, together with several other potential nominees—Freund, Hastie, and Henry Jacob Friendly, a judge on the U.S. Court of Appeals, Second Circuit. It was at lunch yesterday that he made up his mind, the president said, "and then we got our people to call Segal and ask him to poll the twelve members of his committee specifically on Whizzer, as soon as possible. That's what the delay was." (At his 4:00 P.M. briefing the day before, Salinger had told the White House press corps there would be no announcement on the Supreme Court until Monday. Then the White House announced a 5:15 P.M. briefing, which in turn was postponed until 6:30, when Kennedy nominated White.) Segal let the White House know that his committee unanimously endorsed White, and only then—half an hour before the announcement—did the president call White. "I reached him in Denver," Kennedy continued, "and actually he wasn't really enthusiastic. He said he honestly hated to leave the Justice Department, and that's another plus in his favor. He's the ideal New Frontier judge." I said something about White's record in his lifetime being almost too good to be believed . . . like astronaut John Glenn's. "He's a hell of a lot better than John Glenn," the president answered without elaboration.

We next turned to the subject of Teddy Kennedy, whose difficulties with the Harvard authorities had come to light earlier this week.* "I just spoke to him on the phone," the president said. "He feels like he's

---

* In his freshman year at Harvard, Teddy Kennedy had persuaded an undisclosed friend to take a language exam for him. The dean had found them out, and asked both of them to leave college, but with a provision that both could reapply after an absence. After two years in the Army, Teddy Kennedy and friend reapplied and were admitted. They graduated in 1956.

been kicked in the balls, really singing the blues." The story had been kicking around town for a while, and I told the president we had been looking into it for two weeks. Kennedy said, "It was good to get the story out," and went on to add that Teddy had been waiting for the question to be asked when he appeared on "Meet The Press" a few weeks earlier. When I asked the president what effect he thought the cheating scandal would have on Teddy's chances for the Senate nomination, he answered with a real edge in his voice: "It won't go over with the WASPs. They take a very dim view of looking over your shoulder at someone else's exam paper. They go in more for stealing from stockholders and banks."

Still defensively, he asked, "When are you going to send one of your ace reporters to look into Eddie's (McCormack's) record?" I asked him what he meant, and he told me that McCormack had resigned his commission in the Navy on the day he graduated from Annapolis, on a medical disability. "Half of it was nerves and half of it was a bad back," the president drilled on, "and he's been drawing a 60 percent disability ever since up until six months ago.* Dave Powers (now curator of the Kennedy Library in Massachusetts, then "receptionist" at the White House and one of the president's closest friends and admirers) has all the information and he'll give it to you." (I never did talk to Powers about McCormack, but reflected once more on that "Don't-get-mad-get-even" maxim.)

The president seemed basically philosophical about the jam Teddy was in. "He's got six months to fight

---

* McCormack denies Kennedy's statement, claiming that he served in the Navy from June, 1946, until September, 1949, when he resigned to go to law school.

his way out of it," he said. "It's just like my Addison's disease.* It's out, and now he's got to fight it."

The conversation returned to *Newsweek*'s treatment of Jackie's trip, with the president repeating most of the criticism he had voiced two days ago. "When we have distinguished visitors we take them to Mount Vernon; we don't take them to some abandoned coal mine in West Virginia. Ken Galbraith (the Harvard economist and author, then U.S. ambassador to India) told me Jackie took all the bitterness out of our relations with India. If I had gone there, we would have talked about Kashmir and Goa, but Jackie did a helluva job."

Back to Byron White and the Supreme Court, Kennedy recalled that he had first met White in Munich in 1937 or 1938, where White was studying for a few months. He made a point of stressing that the year

---

* Kennedy's Addison's disease was always a mystery to me. It was a not-so-hidden issue in the 1960 campaign, especially in the primary. India Edwards, the onetime Democratic National Committeewoman who was campaigning all-out on behalf of Lyndon Johnson, once told a bunch of reporters that Kennedy was so sick from Addison's disease that he "looked like a spavined hunchback"—one of the least lofty moments of that tense episode. Kennedy's entourage would say only that he had "an adrenal insufficiency." In his book *A Thousand Days*, historian and Kennedy friend Arthur M. Schlesinger, Jr., wrote: "(Kennedy) said that after the war, fevers associated with malaria had produced a malfunctioning of the adrenal glands, but that this had been brought under control." Schlesinger pointed out that Kennedy had none of the symptoms of Addison's disease—yellowed skin, black spots in the mouth, unusual vulnerability to infection—and quoted Kennedy as saying, "No one who has the real Addison's disease should run for the presidency, but I do not have it." Whatever the condition, he did take cortisone derivatives, and when he did, it often made his face fuller. Vain as always, it bugged him if he appeared a little jowly at press conferences, which he often did, not because he overate, but because he was taking some form of cortisone.

CONVERSATIONS WITH KENNEDY

White was the number one ground gainer in professional football, he was also number one in his class at Yale Law School.

On the subject of other judges, the president said that Abe Ribicoff (former and future senator from Connecticut, but then Kennedy's secretary of health, education, and welfare) no longer wanted to be on the Supreme Court and in fact had called him earlier in the week to take himself out of the running. Kennedy did mention Arthur Goldberg favorably, and implied strongly that Goldberg would be on the Supreme Court inevitably. "But not to fill Frankfurter's vacancy," he added. "That's too obvious and cute."

"He's a cheap bastard. That's all . . ."

APRIL 10, 1962 / "Don't you ever work anymore?" said the voice on the telephone, and it was the president calling me at 2:30 in the afternoon. I was home in bed with the flu, the first day of work I'd missed since I'd had polio twenty-five years earlier—and Kennedy knew it.

Kennedy was enthusiastic about a story *Newsweek* had done about the liberals who were criticizing him, wondered who had written it, but was worried about how Arthur Schlesinger would take the paragraph that quoted Kennedy as saying "boy, when those liberals start mixing into policy, it's murder." He asked me "with your well-known tact, to let Arthur know the quote was from someone else, not the president. Tell him it was Kenny" (O'Donnell, the strong, silent, righthand man to JFK, whose scorn for liberals as practical politicians was legendary). With his mouth obviously full of food, he pushed on. "What breaks their ass," he said, referring to the liberals, "is that 78 percent (Kennedy's current popularity index). That really gets them. And who the hell is Oscar Gass? (A liberal quoted in the *Newsweek* piece, Gass was a consulting economist in Washington who had worked in the Treasury Department under FDR.) I asked some of the boys to look him up, and they made him sound like a fifth-rate p.r. man in Jeeb Halaby's (Federal Aviation Agency Chief Najeeb Halaby) outfit. The only one I care about is Joe Rauh. He's great. I've got to have him over. He was with me at least, and he's been a lot of help with the NAACP. On second thought, tell Arthur that the liberal I was talking about was Harlan Cleveland (the Assistant Secretary of State for International Organization Affairs). He'll understand."

When I reminded the president that Cleveland was one of the New Frontier's golden boys last summer, Kennedy said, "Well, it's like Bobby said. He couldn't get rid of his tabloids. He hid them in his cellar." This is a reference to an eight-page tabloid newspaper which was the number one piece of propaganda during the Kennedy campaign. Kennedy volunteers were measured then—and apparently still now—by their ability to distribute copies of this tabloid to houses and apartments in the areas for which they were responsible. It is interesting and significant that success or failure in the distribution still counts today, some eighteen months after the election. I reminded the president that the New Frontiersman I remembered who had the most difficulty getting rid of his tabloid was Bob Wallace (Robert A. Wallace, then an assistant to the secretary of the treasury). "At least he tried," the president said. "He just didn't have it." As a final reference to the story on the liberals, Kennedy suggested that it would have been better if we had quoted him as saying, "When the liberals try to decide policy, it's murder," instead of when they "start mixing into policy"—but he typically made no effort to claim that he had been misquoted.

Turning to the opening day baseball game at which he had presided the day before (Washington Senators 4, Detroit Tigers 1), we talked about the foul ball off the bat of the Senators' Willie Tasby, which had landed about four feet from the president on the corner of the Senators' dugout. "Boy, that sounded like a gun, it was so close," he said. "Take a look at the picture that ran in the *Post* this morning (apparently a picture that showed all members of the presidential party scattering under fire). Dillon (Douglas Dillon, an Eisenhower ambassador to France, now Kennedy's treasury secretary) looks like he's on his way up to testify before the Ways and Means Committee in a hurry. The row behind me is absolutely empty. I sent the picture up to Ev Dirksen with an inscription: 'Where were you Everett?' Dave (Powers) said he would have caught it if he'd brought his glove." The reference to the legendary Dave Powers reminded me that *Newsweek* had scheduled a story on him, and I asked the president for some anecdotes about him. Kennedy told a story about Powers introducing British Prime Minister Harold Macmillan to him as "the greatest name in England," and he recalled Dave referring to Macmillan (in Macmillan's presence) as "the greatest prime minister I ever met"—even though he was quite obviously the one and only prime minister Dave had ever met. (Powers regularly referred to the White

House as "the greatest White House I ever was in," and later told the president that the Shah of Iran was "my kind of Shah.")

The reference to Dirksen prompted me to remind Kennedy of his often-expressed feeling that the Senate minority leader, known as the Wizard of Ooze for his mellifluous, theatrical voice, was "a good guy." The president said he thought Dirksen had been "damned good" and was "damn smart" in backing the UN bond compromise,* putting statesmanship ahead of party politics. "Sid Yates (a liberal Democratic congressman from Illinois, who was running for Dirksen's Senate seat) is screaming."

The conversation turned to journalists—one of the president's all-time favorite subjects. It is unbelievable to an outsider how interested Kennedy was in journalists and how clued in he was to their characters, their office politics, their petty rivalries. I told him that Jim Cannon (former *Newsweek* national editor and special Washington correspondent, now an assistant to Nelson Rockefeller) had gone back to New York and that I was in the market for a couple of good young reporters. "How much do you suppose Tom Wicker makes?" the president asked immediately, referring to one of the leading lights of the *New York Times* Washington bureau and Washington journalism. "And how much could you pay? He wrote a damn good story about my background briefing just before Christmas, the only good story written out of here . . . straight, simple, just

---

* Kennedy had originally asked Congress for authority to buy half of a $200 million UN bond issue to tide the UN over one of its regular financial crises. A bipartisan Senate compromise allowed Kennedy not only to buy the $100 million, but in effect to lend this nation's share of the bonds back to the UN, with the president free to set the interest and duration of the loan.

the way I said it. And then he wrote a helluva story about me and Smathers. It would be a hell of a coup for you to stick it to the *Times* by getting him." I asked him what he thought of Tom Ross, then the number two man in the *Chicago Sun-Times* Washington bureau. The president said "He may have a bit of Dave Wise* in him . . . a bit of a prick, but he's good. I like him and I'd hire him."

I told him of the difficulties we were having trying to see Governor Rockefeller for a *Newsweek* story, and he told me that Charlie Bartlett had gone all the way to Albany, with an appointment, only to be kept waiting for more than an hour, and then put on his coat and left. "You ought to cut Rocky's ass open a little this week," he suggested. He asked who *Newsweek* was betting on as Rockefeller's 1962 opponent. I didn't know much about New York politics, and guessed Wagner (Robert Wagner, the mayor of New York City) was probably the strongest candidate, but the president suggested Screvane (Paul Rogers Screvane, then president of the New York City Council), saying, "He's apparently a hell of an impressive guy." I asked him if he knew something I didn't know, and the president said he did not, but he knew Wagner wanted to run against Ken Keating for the Senate in 1964, and that Rockefeller would probably win anyway, even if he won by a greatly decreased majority. (Rockefeller did win by a comfortable—16 percent—majority.) I said I had heard that pollster Lou Harris was saying the election would be close as hell . . . 10,000 votes either way, but Kennedy said "Old Lou is full of shit on this one."

---

* David Wise was then a political reporter for the *New York Herald Tribune*, later its Washington bureau chief, and now an author.

The president asked if we were going to take a look at Rockefeller's war record. It is interesting how often Kennedy referred to the war records of political opponents. He had often mentioned Eddie McCormack and Hubert Humphrey in this connection, and here now he was at it again with Rockefeller. "Where was old Nels when you and I were dodging bullets in the Solomon Islands?" he wondered aloud. "How old was he? He must have been thirty-one or thirty-two. Why don't you look into that?" Kennedy criticized casually the *New York Herald Tribune* and "Dennison," as he called *Tribune* editor John Denson, my former *Newsweek* boss, and said he believed the paper "was being kept alive only to help Rocky's chances in 1964."

I asked him if he had read *Six Crises*, the book by Nixon about the crises in his life, including his defeat by Kennedy two years ago. "Just the 1960 campaign stuff," Kennedy answered, "and that's all I'm going to read. I can't stand the way he puts everything in Tricia's mouth. It makes me sick. He's a cheap bastard; that's all there is to it."

"I just want to read you a wire"

APRIL 13, 1962 / "It may have been a good week for the Democrats but not for the U.S.," the president started off, when I called him just before lunch to ask about the steel price increases. He was really sore. "Now we are going to have a terrible struggle between management and labor—everything we have been trying to avoid in this administration." Roger Blough (head of U.S. Steel) had just visited Kennedy, and there were rumors before his visit that Big Steel felt it had an understanding on price increases after settling with the steelworkers. "There was no question of any understanding," Kennedy said, his voice raised. "They had to come down here, because they couldn't just have sat up there and not opened their kissers about the increase . . . in the face of reports that steel was going to have a very good year, in the face of steel working at only 80 percent of capacity. And then they come in here two days after the labor contract was signed."

Blough was apparently quiet, as always, not rude or excited. "Perhaps the easiest way I can explain the purpose of my visit," the president quoted Blough as starting the conversation, and then handing the president the statement which had already been given to the newspapers. The president was loath to discuss the details of his conversation with Blough. "I just told him he'd made a terrible mistake." Kennedy was bothered at least as much by the way steel increased its prices as by the price increase itself. "It's the way it was done," he went on. "It looks like such a double cross. I think steel made a deal with Nixon not to raise prices until after the election. Then came the recession, and they didn't want to raise prices. Then when we pulled out of the recession they said, 'Let Kennedy squeeze the unions first, before we raise prices.' So I squeezed McDonald (Dave McDonald, president of the steelworkers union). and gave him a good statesmanship leg to stand on with his workers. And they kicked us right in the balls. And we kicked back. The question really is: are we supposed to sit there and take a cold, deliberate fucking? Is this the way the private enterprise system is really supposed to work? When U.S. Steel says 'Go,' the boys go? How could they all raise their prices almost to a penny within six hours of each other?" I asked Kennedy about the grand jury which the attorney general had convened in New York to look into the price increases, and reports from the business community that it was just a fishing expedition. "I can't go make a speech like I did (Kennedy, on April 11, had called the steel price hike a "wholly unjustifiable and irresponsible defiance of the public interest" and ended his speech by saying, "Some time ago I asked each American to consider what he could do for his country and I asked the steel companies. In the last twenty-four hours we had their answer."), and then sit on my ass," he answered. "They fucked us, and we've got to try to fuck them." I said something about how the political ramifications would probably favor the Democrats. The Democrats could now run against U.S. Steel in November, a pretty good opponent for a Democratic candidate.

"But I don't want that," Kennedy answered. "Everything that we have tried is in the other direction. We want the support of business on trade. We want them on the tax bill. I've been breaking my ass trying to get along with these people. Goldberg (Secretary of Labor Arthur Goldberg) is terribly depressed," the president went on. "He told me 'Shit, I might as well quit. There's nothing I can do now.' We're in for a period in which labor and management are at each other's throats."

The president called me back at 2:00 P.M., when I was lunching at the Hay-Adams with Ken Crawford and Arthur Schlesinger, and he was madder than ever. "I just want to read you a wire," he started off, while

UPI PHOTO

During the steel price crisis of 1962, with Roger Blough of U.S. Steel. The discussions were not easy, and the questions raised in the president's mind were tough. " 'Is this the way the private enterprise system is really supposed to work? When U.S. Steel says "Go," the boys go? How could they all raise their prices almost to a penny within six hours of each other?' "

I signaled the waiter urgently for a pencil and a menu to write on. "It's from the FBI office in New York investigating the steel thing. Quote: 'J. F. Tenant, general counsel United States Steel, informed us today that he is too busy to talk to agents from the bureau.' " And here my notes break down, but the telegram continued to the effect that Tenant suggested to the FBI agent that he be contacted in New York on April 20 (a Friday) for further discussions as to when certain steel company executives might be interviewed by FBI personnel. "Who the fuck do they think they are?" the president asked. "It just shows how smart they think they are and how they think they can screw the government."

The president was about to leave by helicopter from the White House lawn to go on maneuvers with the

Marines, and then on to Palm Beach. But his anger was running over. I asked him about the charges that were being made about his vindictiveness against the steel companies. Kennedy said he'd heard all about them, but asked "what would you have us do? We can go at this thing forty different ways. The point is, I can't just make a charge and then walk away. That's when they say 'We beat 'em.' They used us, that's all, and what can we do? We can't just walk away and lie down. We're going to tuck it to them and screw 'em."

"To Billie Sol Bradlee" or "Better not let that one out of here".

MAY 15, 1962 / The president seemed jumpy and uncomfortable at dinner tonight, perhaps because there were more guests than usual: Chuck and Betty Spalding (he's an old friend and prep school classmate of JFK); Mr. and Mrs. Edward A. McDermott (he's the new director of the Office of Emergency Planning); Frederick "Fritz" Loewe, the composer of Lerner and Loewe fame; Bill Walton and Helen Chavchavadze (a long-time friend of the Kennedys), and ourselves.

Billie Sol Estes was Topic A, the boy wonder from Pecos, Texas who made a fortune in anhydrous ammonia and then got himself indicted and convicted for conspiring to defraud major financial investment firms by selling them non-existent mortgages on non-existent farm equipment. Estes had been loosely tied to Lyndon Johnson, and the *New York Herald Tribune* had come up with a picture of Kennedy and his inaugural address, inscribed to Estes by the president. Kennedy resented the *Tribune* picture, and was making no effort to hide his resentment. *Newsweek* had run the same picture, and we were included in his general unhappiness. "Sixty thousand copies of that document were distributed by the Democratic National Committee," he said aggressively, "none of them actually signed by me, none of them sent to anyone with my particular knowledge." He said the butler was going to bring me in a present from him, and the butler soon did just that. It was the same picture of the president and his inaugural address. In the middle of my dinner, he hauled out a pen and inscribed it "To My Good Friend Billie Sol Bradlee, With Best Regards, John F. Kennedy," and gave it to me right there. But about ten minutes later, as we were getting up from dinner, the president asked for it back, saying, "We better not let that one out of here, I guess."

"But how do you avoid things like the Billie Sol Estes case?" he started speculating. "You kick them out as soon as you find them, but how do you find them, and God knows how many there are.* These

---

* The first Kennedy "scandal," such as it was, involved the jovial and able Frank Reeves, Kennedy's "minorities man" during the campaign, and later a professor of law at Howard University. Frank had forgotten to pay his income taxes, it had been revealed in the newspapers, at a time when he was still on the Kennedy payroll. Kennedy had announced that Reeves would leave the White House immediately, but I had seen him over there a few days after the announcement. I spoke to the president on the telephone a day later and asked him when Reeves was in fact going to leave. "He's left," Kennedy said, sure of himself. I told him how I'd seen him twenty-four hours ago. There was a pause and I could hear the president ask O'Donnell "Is Frank Reeves still around here?" Another pause, then Kennedy back to O'Donnell: "Get his ass out of here, *tonight*."

government departments are like icebergs. People have been dug in there for years." Kennedy reaffirmed, convincingly, his confidence in his secretary of agriculture, Orville Freeman, whose bailiwick included Estes, and his confidence in Freeman's toughness, integrity, and incorruptibility.

Kennedy said he'd received a telephone call recently from Bob Burkhardt (a New Jersey politician), asking the president to sign a picture of himself to one Axel Gottleib. "You can't help but wonder who the hell Axel Gottleib is," he said. "When are we going to indict him?"

Kennedy then told an anecdote I had never heard about his own near-involvement with Bernard Goldfine, the New England textile big spender, for whom Eisenhower's chief of staff Sherman Adams intervened at the Federal Trade Commission (a move that eventually cost Adams his job). "Commissioner (Joseph F.) Timilty (Boston commissioner of police) once asked me to see a guy named Bernard Goldfine the next time I was in Boston. He said Goldfine was a nice guy, contributed to a lot of political campaigns, and surely would contribute to mine. I set up a date to see Goldfine, and then just by accident I had something else to do, so I never saw him. But if I had seen him, I'm sure he would have offered us some financial support, and I'm sure we would have accepted it. At that time no one knew anything against Goldfine. Even so, in 1958, we got a check—unsolicited—from Goldfine for $1,000. Kenny O'Donnell spotted it, remembered that he'd heard some talk about Goldfine being investigated, and Kenny returned the check."

I told Kennedy about how Goldfine once offered—in fact actually gave—me some money, the only person ever to have offered me a dime during my years in this business. I was covering Goldfine's sensational disclosures about his influence before the Legislative Oversight Subcommittee of the House, and was having lunch with him—before 200 witnesses—at the Willard Hotel dining room. In the middle of our conversation Goldfine asked me how many children we had. Six counting stepchildren, I told him, and thereupon, without another word, he pulled out his wallet, plucked out six crisp, new fifty-dollar bills and handed them to me. I said "No" a hundred different ways, but he simply would not take them back. Finally, I held the bills at arm's length and walked over to a nearby table where Goldfine's lawyer, Sam Sears from Boston, was eating, and—again before 200 witnesses—gave them to him.

Conversation turned to Kennedy's remark about all businessmen being sons of bitches, a reaction to the news of the steel price rise. Wallace Carroll had reported in the *New York Times* of April 23, 1962, that the president had said to his advisors April 10, "My father always told me that all businessmen were sons of bitches, but I never believed it till now." The president said tonight "I said sons of bitches, or bastards, or pricks. I don't know which. But I never said anything about *all* businessmen. And furthermore, I called Reston and Reston knows this, but he didn't have the guts to change the original story." The president went on to say that it was bankers and steelmen that his father hated, not all businessmen. But he added that it didn't make much difference now, whether he said all businessmen, or he didn't. The businessmen thought he had, and that was fine with him . . . "wherever you are."

Kennedy fingered his elaborately scripted place card at one point during dinner, and said out of the blue that he had a collection of these place cards signed by every head of state who had been honored at a White House dinner. The collection now amounts to some sixty cards, he said, as pleased as a small child talking about his bug collection.

I sat next to Ann Gargan, the Kennedy cousin who made a life's work out of taking care of the president's father. She painted a pathetic picture of "Uncle Joe," saying that apparently his mind works perfectly—or almost perfectly—but that he still cannot talk after his stroke. She told me she telephoned him at least once a day whenever she was away from him, which is not often. Apparently she just rambles on, while he just mumbles unintelligible noises. We also chatted about her memories of "Honey Fitz," Kennedy's legendary grandfather who had been the mayor of Boston. Kennedy interrupted to observe that Honey Fitz's day was long gone.

At one point the president got off on France and de Gaulle, how difficult de Gaulle was, how difficult it would be to find his replacement, and then he digressed on the French economy, which he said he had been studying. "It's fascinating," he said. "Here's a country getting a 5½ percent annual increase in its GNP, while we struggle to get 2½ percent. They have almost no unemployment, while we have too much." Kennedy then revealed that he had asked Walter Heller, the chairman of his Council of Economic Advisors, to send some CEA staffers to France for a report on how France was able to do it.

"You want to read something fantastic?"

MAY 16, 1962 / We were back at the White House for dinner this night, this time with Ziggy de Segonzac (Adalbert de Segonzac, long-time Washington correspondent of *France-Soir*) and his wife. There was a slight interruption just before dinner, when Nancy called to announce that our house was on fire. I called the fire department from the White House, and rushed back to find the street blocked by fire engines, and my heart sank. But it was only the dishwasher motor, smoking, and I was back before the cocktail hour was over.

The president drinks at least one Scotch on these occasions, but often doesn't have a second, even though the guests do. He walks in after everyone has arrived usually, a little stiff at first, it seems, immaculately dressed (and often quite critical of my clothes. I remember wearing brown shoes—dark, dark brown shoes—with a blue suit one night, and he went out of his way to tell me that the combination was out; okay for daytime, but never at night.). He loosens up as the evening wears on. He likes to tease, loves to be teased, especially by Jackie, when she calls him "Bunny."

Kennedy walked into the Oval Room, and even before ordering a drink, pulled a two-page cable out of his pocket and asked us "You want to read something fantastic?" and started reading aloud. It was a cable, presumably to the Pentagon from some low-ranking

Army officer in the American military mission in Vientiane, Laos, and the tone was one of indignant frustration. "We're still holding Houei Sai, but no thanks to the Royal Laotian Army, whose performance is just plain gutless," the president read. "While the battle for the airstrip was raging, the Royal Laotian forces were swimming in a nearby stream." The president broke off reading the cable to report that two Laotian generals had evacuated Nam Sa before the twelve-man U.S. mission had evacuated. General Phoumi (Phoumi Nosavan, deputy premier of Laos) was a "total shit," Kennedy said, and he was particularly annoyed at Phoumi's trip yesterday to see Chiang Kai Shek in Formosa.

The subject switched to the Adenauer-Rusk and the Adenauer-Kennedy letters. The State Department was sore because some of the U.S. proposal for the Berlin negotiations, which we had been discussing with our allies, had leaked. With suspicion, but without proof that a German official was involved in the leak, Rusk had sent the German foreign secretary an apparently sharp note, and that in turn annoyed Adenauer, who had written Kennedy. "Rusk's letter had been tough," the president said, and along the lines of "we know something about leaks, but this is no way to resolve as difficult a problem as this one." Kennedy said his own letter to Adenauer had been slightly more mollifying, but making the point that the U.S. wanted to go to the mat with Adenauer for something substantive, not just details of a problem. The president was now mad at Wilhelm Grewe, the German ambassador in Washington, who was obviously suspected of responsibility for the leak. "Either he doesn't speak English," Kennedy said, "or something is seriously wrong with him." Kennedy was referring to some statement Grewe had made about how bilateral talks had been helpful and how he expected both sides would soon be changing their positions. When Ziggy told Kennedy that Grewe had been perhaps a little friendlier with the Nazis than he should have been, Kennedy was delighted. "That explains it," he said . . . simplistically.

There was a general discussion about the recent most successful visit to Washington of André Malraux (writer, philosopher, Resistance hero, and de Gaulle's minister of state in charge of cultural affairs). Jackie was particularly enthusiastic, saying that he was the first French official who wasn't bored to tears by protocol. She quoted Malraux as saying to Kennedy as they rose to meet the first guests at the White House reception in his honor, "maintenant au travail." There was quite a bit of French spoken during the evening, in honor of Ziggy and Malraux's visit. For some reason it bugs Kennedy that I speak French.

Kennedy finds it intolerable that he doesn't have the facility for languages that others have, and his pride in Jackie's linguistic talents is tinged with jealousy and bewilderment. His French can only be described as unusual. One French friend says he speaks it "with a bad Cuban accent," while another says, "He apparently doesn't believe in French verbs, much less pronounce them correctly." Just before his trip to Berlin in June, 1963, he spent the better part of an hour with the Vreelands (Frederick "Frecky" Vreeland, a young foreign service officer and the son of *Vogue* editor Diana Vreeland, and his wife) before he could master "Ich bin ein Berliner."

I told Kennedy about the tragedy of Tom Streithorst, *Newsweek*'s Middle East correspondent. Tom and his Lebanese bride had been driving through Turkey on their honeymoon when they collided head-on with a truck. Tom's wife had been killed in the accident, and the Turks had slapped him into some village jail on charges of murdering his wife via the accident. "The Turks are mean bastards," Kennedy said. "I remember reading somewhere how they never took prisoners during their wars. They just hammered their shoes onto their heels with long spikes and let them go." Kennedy was obviously moved by Streithorst's trauma, and volunteered to help. "I'd hate to think of this guy in jail or staying in jail if there was anything I could do to spring him." We were trying to spring him through embassies in Washington and Ankara, and I told him so, but asked if I could solicit his help if we needed it. He said "absolutely." (Streithorst finally was released on bail, but had to flee the country to avoid being tried for murder.)

We next talked about my friend Claude Cheysson, and I asked the president if he would see this extraordinary Frenchman, who had been my friend in Paris. (Cheysson is now commissioner for development of the European Community, but was then a young French foreign service officer, about to be named director general of the Sahara Authority. No matter how extraneous to his own experience or unknown to the general public, Kennedy liked to meet friends of his friends, provided they were involved in vital fields—"out there on the cutting edge," he once called it. The president did in fact see Cheysson for one hour—instead of the scheduled fifteen minutes—two days later. Cheysson has since given me his written impressions of that conversation.)

Washington, 1962

There was some excitement in the voice of the

porter of the small hotel where I was staying in Washington in the fall of 1962 when he told me "the president will receive you tomorrow at the White House at 6 P.M." But there was much more surprise when I heard the news. I had come to the States for interviews with the AID and the National Science Foundation; nothing justified a call by such an important person.

One hour later, my friend Ben Bradlee gave me the clue. He had told the president that some unknown French friend of his had had very close contact with the nationalist movements in North Africa and was now in a unique position to travel throughout black Africa and therefore to know something of this little-known continent where some thirty countries were engaged in a process of independence. The president felt that important changes were to be expected in Africa. He was anxious to express the American sympathy for these newborn or almost-born countries.

That Friday afternoon I was introduced in the oval room, and two minutes later we were in the thick of it. No time had been wasted in useless words of courtesy. "I am interested in Africa," JFK said. "I know little about it. Our people have little direct experience. I want you to tell me how you see things, in the countries themselves and in relation with the European interests, misgivings, and ambitions."

There were just the two of us. The president was swinging slowly in his familiar arm chair. He was listening intensely, speaking very little, just to ask an additional question, or to be sure that he had understood well what I meant. We spent almost one hour together, no one interrupted, the telephone never rang.

The questions were sometimes surprising to a foreigner, a man with limited responsibility. As soon as the president knew how I felt, he passed to another point.

The simplicity of the style was amazing: "Do you think communism is going to progress fast when the countries become independent?" JFK asked me.

"Mr. President, what do you call communism in a developing country which has no political structure to be compared with ours. . . ?" I had no time to end my sentence, the president interrupted: "It is a stupid question. I withdraw it. Tell me if you feel the Russians are really interested and how you think they will play their game." And we discussed Soviet policies in Africa, most objectively, coming to the conclusion for instance that the United States should next to the USSR be very active in a country like Guinea, because the trauma of the break with France was serious, the country was potentially wealthy and had a very impressive leader.

When we considered North Africa (Morocco and Tunisia had just become independent, Algeria was in the thick of war), we wasted no time discussing whether Algeria would become independent, but discussed how it. could be helped immediately afterwards, and how relations, friendly relations, could be promoted with France after independence. The president was obviously impressed by the personality of General de Gaulle, but he also wanted Algeria to be successful; therefore he wondered what could be done, then and later, what kind of a first American ambassador should be appointed.

Many problems were discussed under such a personal approach. The president felt that his representative in an emerging country should give the proper image of the American people, should do much more than report facts, should be a natural intermediary between the two parties. One point illustrated this approach: "I have been advised to send Negro Americans as diplomats to black Africa. How do you feel?" Embarrassing question for a young and modest visitor. Still I spoke against the idea, stressing that a foreign country expects to receive an envoy who really represents the state and that some Africans might feel slighted if they did not have the same type of American ambassadors as the Italians, Swedes, or Indians. The president immediately agreed.

The purpose of the interview was not for JFK to tell me about the American policy; he was not anxious to speak, to convince; he wanted to listen, to hear, and that he did most remarkably. Very seldom in my life have I been listened to so well.

At the end of the meeting, the president called his secretary and dictated a summary of our conversation. He checked that I agreed; I corrected one word. He ordered that the note be sent to various people in the White House and the Department of State; he also instructed his secretary to tell McGeorge Bundy to arrange a meeting the next day to clarify one point, go deeper into two subjects. Then, most kindly but very briefly he bade me farewell. He had been listening; he had heard enough. His mind was already elsewhere, even if his kind attention was still with me.

I left the place under his charm, of course. But I was very impressed also that the most powerful man in the world had managed to take one hour in his time on a Friday afternoon to hear —from someone unknown and insignificant—news and impressions about a problem that was not urgent, but a problem which bore on the independence, on the liberty, and the progress of countries and people.   —C. Cheysson

There was some miscellaneous conversation next— how well Gavin (General James Gavin, then U.S. ambassador to France and an early Kennedy supporter, now head of Arthur D. Little Co.) was doing in Paris, how difficult de Gaulle was (again), how unrealistic was his request for atomic weapons, and how he had refused even a token French contribution to SEATO for Laos. And then we went downstairs to the White House theater under the East Wing to watch a twenty-minute movie short which had been made of the president's recent examination of U.S. naval strength. Only average, I thought, but Kennedy seemed moved. The most striking thing to me about the screening was the bed which has been recently moved into the theater. It's in the front row of seats, its back raised, with four pillows. Kennedy said his back had been giving him extra trouble, and he had had to watch movies from the bed. But he was in his rocking chair tonight, and said his back felt better, enough better so that he hoped to play golf in September.

On the way back upstairs he took us through the swimming pool, which is something else. A French artist, Bernard Lamott, is painting murals on three sides of the pool, from top tile to ceiling, and the fourth wall is a mirror. The effect is one of being totally surrounded by a subtropical seascape harbor. The president pointed with pride to a white blob in the middle of the harbor, and announced proudly that it was going to be the *Honey Fitz*, the presidential yacht renamed for his grandfather. (The pool was boarded over in 1969 at President Nixon's direction— and how *that* would have annoyed JFK—the murals are in storage, awaiting completion of the Kennedy Library.)

The president announced before going to bed that the June party was now definitely scheduled . . . for June 3, but instead of the usual hundred guests, this one was going to be limited to "about thirty-five real swingers . . . none of those bastards from New York."

"Everyone's going mad up there"

MAY 30, 1962 / I called the president in Glen Ora just after noon to wish him a happy birthday, one day late, and he felt like talking . . . mostly about the stock market and his relationships to the business community. He said William McChesney Martin (head of the Federal Reserve System) had told him early this year that two acts by the administration would improve relationships with business more than anything else. One was a balanced budget, and the other was a quick, non-inflationary steel settlement. "We submitted a balanced budget," he said, "even if we did have to stretch it a bit, and we got an early, non-inflationary steel settlement. I think that when steel raised its prices everybody felt that we were going to have more inflation, and so the market looked good. When we stepped in against steel, what we were really doing was giving business the sound dollar it had always wanted. But that meant *no* inflation, and so the wild ride of the stock market started." Kennedy said he felt "now was a good time for me to shut up. I've told business I love them. There's no sense telling them I love them any more. They don't believe it. Fuck 'em. It's like Peter the Hermit's day. Everyone's going mad up there." (Peter the Hermit was an eleventh-century monk who set out for Palestine with 30,000 undisciplined followers. They became so unruly that Peter tossed in the towel and joined the army of Godfrey de Bouillon and helped capture Jerusalem.)

"I've reminded Bill Martin of what he told me earlier this year," Kennedy went on, noting that margin rates were set by the Federal Reserve, not by him. "I said to him, 'The Fed has a piece of this policy, and don't you forget it.' "

Philosophically, Kennedy worried out loud about the widening gap between the people who can discuss the complicated issues of today with intelligence and knowledge, and those he later referred to as "the conservative community." It is a theme that fascinates him, and one to which he returns time and time again: a kind of Dialogue of the Deaf, growing and disturbing, between that comparative handful of people truly knowledgeable about the increasingly complex issues of our society, and the great majority who just don't understand these issues and hide their lack of understanding behind the old clichés. (He made an important speech on the subject at Yale University. It was never far from his thoughts).

"There never has been so big a gap between the actual issues and discussions of these issues. I even talked to Malraux about this when he was here. The trouble is that the problems are so complicated and so technical that only a handful of people really understand them, and so the average man discussing these problems falls back on a bunch of outdated, if not meaningless, slogans like 'sound dollar,' and 'fiscal integrity,' and these old slogans are losing their value. The dialogue between the conservative community and the president has become a terrible problem." Without complete information, which is necessarily limited to a few because of the complexities of any given problem, he continued, the average American is forced to rely for information on what he reads. "And the publications they read are so weighted to please them, it's really disturbing."

This led us, as always, into today's discussion of the frailties of the press. We talked at some length about his recent cancellation of twenty-four White House subscriptions to the *New York Herald Tribune,* ordered in a fit of pique.* He obviously relished whatever displeasure he was causing the *Tribune,* and equally obviously was oblivious to the criticism of his act as demeaning and petty. "Did you know that Dennison (for Denson, the *Tribune* editor) ordered Bob

---

* The cancellation was not the most effective embargo in the history of the presidency. Most of the White House subscribers, like Arthur Schlesinger, simply picked up their copies at newsstands like "Doc" Dalinsky's Georgetown Pharmacy, until the foolishness of the order was obvious and the cancellation was rescinded.

Kennedy gave the cancellation order to Jack McNally, a low-level employee in the White House transportation department, and McNally carried it out. Salinger said later he would not have carried it out, if the president had ordered him to cancel the subscriptions.

Donovan to file a protest and to find out why the cancellations?" he asked. "Old Jock (John Hay Whitney, former ambassador to the Court of St. James under President Eisenhower, and owner of the *Herald Tribune*) is just keeping it alive to help Rockefeller in 1964," he said. "The trouble is, no one will buy it then; it will be too late. Why don't you get Phil Graham to buy the *Tribune* Syndicate? That's all they've got." The straw that broke his back, he said, came the day after Senator Stuart Symington's investigation of stockpiling policies had revealed the multi-million-dollar copper windfall arranged for by Messrs. George M. Humphrey, Arthur S. Flemming, and Robert B. Anderson, all members of Eisenhower's cabinet, whose fingerprints were all over the copper stockpile. Symington had revealed that the U.S. had lost nearly one billion dollars, and that some producers had made profits of 700 percent to 1000 percent. "And those bastards didn't have a line on it," Kennedy said, referring to the *Tribune*. "Not a goddamn line. We read enough shit. We just don't have to read that particular brand."

I told the president I was going up to Springfield, Mass., for the state Democratic convention where Teddy Kennedy was making his political debut, trying to win the nomination for senator from Eddie McCormack, and said I'd heard from his boys that Teddy seemed to have it sewed up.

"That's what they tell me," the president said, "but I haven't seen the arithmetic this time. And they have a couple of question marks that I wonder about next to some delegates. Specifically, after Mayor Brennan's name (Cyril K. Brennan of Attleboro, Mass.). They had a question mark after his name until they picked up the paper and read his speech knocking the hell out of Teddy. If they have too many of those kinds of question marks, maybe it isn't sewed up so tight." He said Speaker McCormack was being very polite to him, but "he won't talk to O'Brien, he's just barely civil to O'Donnell, and he's doing a lot of telephoning. We know that."

The president then paused briefly to take a whack at "that Philippine son of a bitch," referring to Diosdado Macapagal (elected president of the Philippines in 1961), and "that bastard de Gaulle." Macapagal, he revealed, had also refused to send even a token force to Southeast Asia. "When we finally persuaded him to send sixty men—sixty goddamn men—he said only on one condition: that the Thais refuse." De Gaulle, he said, had refused even to send a single airplane, even though France was a member of SEATO.

Newsweek had decided to send a reporter to Europe, as a result, really, of Kennedy's fascination, to explore the reasons for the French and German economic successes. He was quickly interested, suggested we send Bart Rowen (Hobart Rowen, then *Newsweek*'s business and financial man in Washington, later business and financial editor of the *Washington Post*), and came up with several story ideas. "Ask Bart to look at what's happened to the European market in the last year. Bill Martin came back the other day, convinced the bloom is off the European boom, and told me that the German market is off 30 percent in the last eighteen months."

And this economic discussion brought him back to the whole question of the relationship between his administration and business. He told me about a man who was mediating a settlement between the fabricators of steel and the steel union, giving the union the line about responsibility and non-inflation, when Blough announced his price rise. "This guy told me that the union members who had been willing to settle for a dime, heard the news and came storming in to him and said, 'Don't give us that responsibility horseshit. We're going for a quarter now.'" The president summed up: "If we hadn't held the line on steel, we'd have the damnedest inflation ever, right now."

I told him that a *Newsweek* stringer in Texas was working on the murder in Texas of a man named Marshall, who had been investigating the Billie Sol Estes case. (Henry H. Marshall, an agent for the Agricultural Stabilization and Conservation Service, was found dead in June, 1961, with five bullets in him from his own rifle. Originally police called it a suicide, but later changed their verdict to murder.) The stringer was telling *Newsweek* that the murder was not involved with the Billie Sol Estes investigation, but was tied directly to an extra-curricular romance. Kennedy was all ears, wanting to know whether the murder had been committed by the husband or the brother, asked me how we had learned about the case, and urged me to call the attorney general. (I didn't since it was a holiday, but Bobby Kennedy called me that night at 8:30.) "That explains it perfectly," Kennedy concluded, "and to think those bastards on the *Herald Tribune* must have known this and were still writing it as a Billie Sol case."

"Don't worry. Just call collect"

JUNE 8, 1962 / In the middle of the hectic first ballot
at the Massachusetts Democratic convention in Springfield, a girl I had never seen before gave me a message
to call Operator 18 in Washington. It was about 9:30
P.M., and I placed the call from a pay phone on the
press table in front of me. I figured it had to be Tony
with some child in trouble, but it was the president, of
all the people, asking me how things were going.
Apparently he had been unable to get through to
Steve Smith, his brother-in-law, who was running the
convention operation for Teddy, and he'd just picked up
the telephone and asked those incredible White House
telephone operators to "get me Ben Bradlee, please; he's
at the Democratic convention in Springfield."* He was
looking for up-to-the-minute information on Teddy's
status—which was good. I read him the final predictions Steve Smith had given me just before the balloting
started, plus the actual votes in the four or five districts
which had already been polled. "About eight percent

---

* Kennedy was justly proud of the uncanny ability of the
White House telephone operators to find anyone, anywhere,
at any time of the day or night. Once, he dared Tony and
Jackie and me to come up with a name of someone the operators couldn't find. Jackie suggested Truman Capote, because
he had an unlisted telephone number. Kennedy picked up the
telephone and said only "Yes, this is the president. Would you
please get me Truman Capote?"—no other identification. Thirty
minutes later, Capote was on the line . . . not from his own
unlisted number in Brooklyn Heights, but at the home of a
friend in Palm Springs, Calif., who also had an unlisted number.

slippage," Kennedy noted quickly, "and that's not bad." He was completely familiar with all the districts, and the individual delegates as they were polled. I described to him how Peter "Leather Lungs" Clougherty was even now approaching the podium to tell John Powers (the state senator, later mayor of Boston, who was presiding) that someone in some delegation had just questioned the vote and was demanding that the delegation be polled. "He's a real bastard—Clougherty," the president said. "Took me for two or three thousand dollars once. Cashed some checks of mine during one campaign." He asked how Eddie McCormack was doing, and I said I found him likable and articulate —for a Massachusetts pol. But I told him what depressed me about Eddie was the people around him . . . men like Patrick J. "Sonny" McDonough, Clougherty, and Knocko McCormack (Edward J. McCormack, Sr., brother of the Speaker and father of the candidate),* and others like them. The president agreed, making the point he had made before about his grandfather. "Their day is gone, and they don't know it." He asked about his younger brother, and I said I couldn't see much difference in the quality of the delegates loyal to Teddy and loyal to Eddie, but certainly the people

---

* McDonough and McCormack were right out of *The Last Hurrah*. My father used to tell—with delight—a story about a time when he was chairman of the Massachusetts Parole Commission. Sonny McDonough appeared before the commission with a convict whose request for parole Sonny was about to present. As my father walked in to take his seat, he heard Sonny lean over to his client and say "Jeez, we're out of luck. Bradlee just showed up. He pisses ice water."

Knocko used to run a saloon in Dorchester, and was particularly active on election day. For this occasion, he had thousands of slips of paper printed up, with "OK, Knocko" written on them. And it was said that if a man voted Knocko's way, he would receive two "OK Knocko"s for his pains, good for two free drinks in Knocko's saloon the next day.

running Teddy's campaign were of a generally superior quality. I said that most of the delegates seemed to me in the middle of this evening to be squalid, stewed, and generally second-rate.

Kennedy then said a friend of mine would like to talk to me, and it was Tony, but in a short time he was back on the telephone for another check. A delegation was being polled, and he asked if I could call him back in half an hour or so. I said I didn't have enough change to finance the call from the pay booth, and he said simply "Don't worry; just call collect." I guess I was spoiled, but not that spoiled, and I couldn't help wondering about the reaction of some of my colleagues sitting beside me at the press table . . . Carleton Kent of the *Chicago Sun-Times*, Bob Healy of the *Boston Globe,* Mary McGrory of the *Washington Star,* and Doug Cater of the *Reporter* magazine . . . if they had known who was getting the collect call from the *Newsweek* man. Not to mention some of Eddie McCormack's musclemen just beneath me on the convention floor. When I did call him back, about 10:45, he had obviously been in recent contact with Steve Smith, because he had the latest ballot information, and so we talked generally about Massachusetts politics, and I passed on some miscellany that I'd picked up in cruising the convention floor (Eddie was mad at "them S.O.B.'s in the Lynn Chamber of Commerce"; Teddy was criticized for having a short fuse, although the delegates pronounced it "shot fuse").

The president typically asked how I was going to write the lead of my story, and said, "It almost has to be something about the First Hurrah, doesn't it?" This annoyed me, since I had already written my lead on the plane flying up to Boston ("For fledgling politician Edward Moore Kennedy, 30, the First Hurrah rose

101

from a steaming, smoking auditorium in Springfield, Mass., at 12:25 A.M., June 9, 1962"), though in fairness he had given me the title *The First Hurrah* for a book I had once thought of writing about his first hundred days as president. I guess to get even I made a point of telling him I was planning to use a quotation from Mark Anthony deWolfe Howe (a Harvard law professor who had opposed Teddy's candidacy) to the effect that it was "preposterous and insulting for Teddy Kennedy to ask the voters to boost him from nowhere to the United States Senate." This didn't seem to bother him a bit, but he launched into a pitch for Teddy based on the fact that he was a young and "untainted" candidate who could win and who could give Massachusetts for the first time a united Democratic party. I said that might be true, but only if he could get decent people on the ballot with him, specifically Endicott "Chub" Peabody (who did get on the ballot with Teddy and later became governor of Massachusetts). I wondered whether Peabody could make it, because I had never seen so much obvious racial and religious feeling outside of the South. With Peabody in his hotel room, off the convention floor, I told Kennedy, I felt mighty lonely. He laughed, and said "You're probably the only WASP around."

Tony reported later that it had been a gay evening at the White House, with just the president, Jackie, Bill Walton, and herself. Walton had called her from the White House at the last minute, asking her to join him at "the Pizza Palace on Pennsylvania Avenue." A lot of general gaiety, and a little "twist," apparently. Walton was being pressured by Jackie to succeed the retiring David Finley as chairman of the Fine Arts Commission. And he was resisting this pressure, feeling that he would lose his identity as an artist. (Two days later he got a long, handwritten letter from Jackie, pointing out to him how she had been able to organize her life and still keep her identity and privacy.) There was also talk of how the Kennedys might lose Glen Ora, the lovely place outside Middleburg, Virginia, which they liked. They are apparently trying to work out some arrangement whereby the owner, Mrs. Raymond Tartière, has it most of the time, but makes it available occasionally to the Kennedys.

"Bobby and I smile sardonically"

JUNE 14, 1962 / The president was in a particularly gay and effusive mood last night, while other Kennedys —Bobby, Pat Lawford, Ethel, and Jean Kennedy Smith —were critical in one way or another of last week's stories, especially mine—about Teddy's nomination. They all felt any discussion of a Kennedy dynasty was unfair. The occasion was a party given for the president by Jean and Steve Smith. Jean was particularly horrified when I told her *Newsweek* was planning a Kennedy dynasty cover story—with pictures of JFK, Bobby, and Teddy on the cover—if Teddy won the primary and election. She was truly appalled, and asked if I'd still do the story if the president refused to cooperate. I was so sure he would cooperate that I agreed to her suggestion that we ask him for the family line on whether or not the Kennedy dynasty was a legitimate area of inquiry for a responsible national newsmagazine. Jean bet me he would have some qualification, and she was right, but not the way she had thought. "After he's elected," Kennedy said. "The idea's not only legitimate, but fascinating."

About 10:30 P.M. the president stood up to make a toast, excusing himself for beginning in Jean's absence (she returned a few minutes later, announcing to all concerned "Sorry, kid, I had to go peeps"), but he said he had to watch the rebroadcast of his news conference at 11:00. He wanted to make a toast to the attorney general, he said, and went on to describe how he had been talking that afternoon with Jim Patton, president of Republic Steel. "I was telling Patton what a son of a bitch he was," the president said with a smile, referring obliquely to his now famous remark that all businessmen were sons of bitches. He waited with that truly professional sense of timing instinctive to the best comedians, and went on ". . . and he was proving it. Patton asked me 'Why is it that all the telephone calls of all the steel executives in all the country are being tapped?' And I told him that I thought he was being wholly unfair to the attorney general and that I was sure that it wasn't true. And he asked me 'Why is it that all the income tax returns of all the steel executives in all the country are being scrutinized?' And I told him that, too, was wholly unfair, that the attorney general wouldn't do any such thing. And then I called the attorney general and asked him why he was tapping the telephones of all the steel executives and examining the tax returns of all the steel executives . . . and the attorney general told me that was wholly untrue and unfair." And then another Stanislavsky pause. "And of course, Patton was right."

At this point Bobby interrupted from the floor to explain in mock seriousness: "They were mean to my brother. They can't do that to my brother."

There was a great deal of conversation about Teddy. The president wanted to hear all the stories from Springfield—preferably in dialect. At one point, Bobby asked me to rise to drink a toast to Teddy, on the grounds that I had been the only one present who was in Massachusetts when he won the nomination. The Kennedys—not JFK or Jackie—have a habit of urging people to get on their feet and make inappropriate speeches, only to drown them out with catcalls when they do. It seemed to me now that they were somehow trying to get me to commit myself to his candidacy and more generally to his virtue, and I didn't want to play that game. The president made a big point of saying that Teddy had to win three separate victories—the convention, the primary, and the election—and that in working for these three victories, he would qualify himself as a senator. He seemed convinced that any thirty-year-old who could survive three such difficult fights was qualified by the very fact of his victories. Kennedy criticized the *Time* story of Teddy's nomination with its heavy dose of Knocko McCormack, and made the point that Knocko's significance lay in the fact that he had no significance. He particularly objected to a phrase in the *Time* piece that had Teddy smiling "sardonically."

"Bobby and I smile sardonically," he said with a smile. "Teddy will learn how to smile sardonically in two or three years, but he doesn't know how, yet."

Kennedy was pleased that Chub Peabody had been nominated for governor. He makes it obvious that he does not particularly admire Peabody . . . "He's not long on brains" . . . but he thinks that Peabody's wife is good, that Peabody is "a helluva worker" with a good chance to beat John Volpe. (He did, by 3091 votes.) Reform in Massachusetts politics, Kennedy

"He particularly objected to a phrase in the Time piece that had Teddy smiling 'sardonically.'

" 'Bobby and I smile sardonically,' he said with a smile. 'Teddy will learn how to smile sardonically in two or three years, but he doesn't know how, yet.' "

said, would have to be instituted by the governor, "and of course Bobby is the one who could have done the job better than anybody."

At about 11:00 P.M. I got the president alone for a few minutes to explore how *Newsweek* might expand his Yale speech on the crippling myths of America into a "violin" for next week's issue. ("Violin" is the term used by newsmagazines for the thematic, opening section of the magazine.) He was very interested, and ticked off a whole series of what he called myths . . . that massive retaliation was any longer a viable policy; that failure to recognize a foreign country somehow made that country suffer. He said that some myths were obviously still too sacred to discuss publicly, at least for him to discuss. He warned me not to attribute to him a conviction that the failure of the United States to recognize Red China was a mistake. But he said I could say that Washington was reexamining many myths, including that one.

I asked him who was going to be the new American ambassador to Moscow. "It won't be Ken Galbraith," he answered. "We've got to get a man who speaks Russian. A little give and take is so important." Reinhardt (G. Frederick Reinhardt, then ambassador to Italy) and Kohler (Foy D. Kohler, then assistant secretary of state for European affairs) were the two career foreign service candidates, he said. (Kohler got it.) And he steered me off a report we had heard that he had found a non-career candidate and talked to him earlier in the week.

"Oh, hi. How've you been?"

SEPTEMBER 14, 1962 / I saw the president in Newport briefly this morning, for the first time since I had been banished for my part in the *Look* magazine critique of the Kennedys and the press. We exchanged an absolute minimum of words over an elapsed time of perhaps twenty minutes. I was greeted with "Oh, hi. How've you been?" In the middle of the "conversation," he said "That's fine" a couple of times. And at the end, he asked after Tony and said, "See you later."

I had been nervous about seeing him again——after three months in the doghouse. In a strange way, I understood why he was sore . . . it was hard to make new friends once those White House doors had closed behind you, and if old friends wanted to be friends *and* reporters, maybe the two couldn't mix. I wanted to be friends again. I missed the access, of course, but I missed the laughter and the warmth just as much. What I couldn't and wouldn't do was send a message over the stone wall, saying I had learned my lesson. Anyway, the freeze is obviously still on.

The occasion for this brief encounter was the sequel, at last, of the case of "John's Other Wife." Most Washington correspondents, or at least most of those with any involvement in covering the White House, had been familiar with the broad outlines of the case for months. And yet no responsible newspaper or magazine had written one word about it.

Some anti-Semitic, racist hate sheets had published

108

stories, however ("Kennedy's Divorce Exposed! Is Present Marriage Valid? Excommunication Possible"), and I felt *Newsweek* could be first with the story if we backed into it by writing about the hate sheets themselves in the Press section, how they were spreading the story, and who was financing them. I approached Salinger with the idea, but told him I would need some solid FBI documentation about the character of the organizations and people involved in spreading the Blauvelt story.

A couple of days later, Salinger called me with the following proposition: If I agreed to show the president the finished story, and if I got my tail up to Newport where he was vacationing, he would deliver a package of the relevant FBI documents to a Newport motel and let me have them for a period not to exceed twenty-four hours. It was specifically understood that I was not to xerox anything in the FBI files, that I was not to indicate in any way that I had been given access to FBI files (I never had been given such access before, and I have never been given such access since), and that in case of a lawsuit, I would not be given access to these files a second time. I checked with *Newsweek*'s editor, Oz Elliott, and we decided to go ahead, despite a reluctance to give anyone, even the president of the United States, the right of approval of anything we wrote. In effect, we were giving Kennedy what he later said he liked so much, "the right of clearance." This is a right all presidents covet, but which they should normally not be given. This one time, the book seemed worth the candle, however, and we decided to strike the deal.

Chuck Roberts, *Newsweek*'s White House correspondent, and I got on the next plane to Newport via Providence, and went right to the motel. The FBI files arrived soon afterwards, late in the afternoon, and we stayed up all night long, first reading everything in the files, then writing the story.

"Ever since the heyday of yellow journalism," the story in the magazine's Press section began, "the sense of responsibility of the American press has been more censured than praised. For political profit or for readers' pennies, sensation has often triumphed over reliability.

"But for the last 16 months, virtually every major newspaper, magazine and wire service in the U.S. has refused to publish a sensational report—familiar to hundreds of thousands of Americans—about the president of the United States. They have spiked the story despite what appears to be 'documentary evidence' and despite scattered publication of it, or hints at it, by hate groups and gossip columnists.

"The 'story' falsely alleges that before he married Jacqueline Bouvier in Newport, R.I., on Sept. 12, 1953, John F. Kennedy was secretly married to a two-time divorcee."

The story went on to describe the organizations that were spreading the story . . . an Alabama hate sheet called "The Thunderbolt"; an Arkansas racist sheet called "The Winrod Letter," which had distributed hundreds of thousands of specially photostated four-page folders entitled "The Blauvelt Family Genealogy"; the Christian Education Association, headed by Condé McGinley, publisher of what the FBI called "the vitriolic hate sheet 'Common Sense' "; the "Right Brigade," described by Cleveland police as a "crackpot" organization; and a Holyoke, Mass., paper company whose mailings were handled by an associate of Robert Welch, founder of the John Birch Society.

At eight o'clock the next morning, as planned, I took

the finished piece over to Hammersmith Farm, the Auchincloss summer mansion, where the Kennedys were vacationing to watch the America's Cup races, returned the FBI files to Salinger, and got the president's ok. As I was leaving his office with Kennedy, we bumped into the Ormsby-Gores, who were joining the Kennedys to watch the yacht races. The British ambassador smiled politely and asked if I were joining them for the races.

"No," Kennedy answered quickly. "He's not coming." And he meant it.

Lollipops

NOVEMBER 6, 1962 / Maybe the exile is ending.

Jackie invited Tony over to the White House to play tennis today, and then invited the children over for movies and supper.

Just before leaving, the whole clan—Tony, Jackie, and a total of seven children—trooped down to the president's office, shouting, screaming, and licking lollipops.

The lollipops were given to Arthur Schlesinger to hold while Marina and John did their special dance at the request of the president.

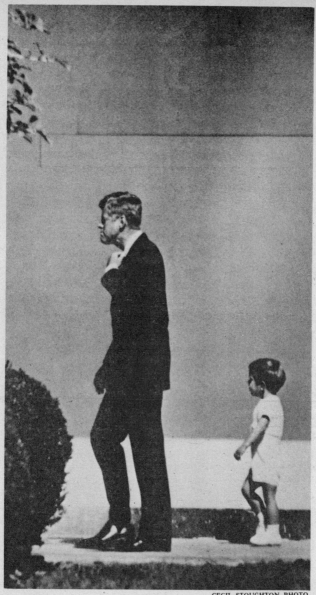

CECIL STOUGHTON PHOTO

Everybody loves everybody again

NOVEMBER 9, 1962 / There was a dance at the White House tonight, smaller than any of the others, about sixty people. This was the one that had been scheduled for June. We had cocktails upstairs in the Oval Room, dinner and dancing downstairs in the Blue Room.

The president and Tony had a long session about the difficulties of being friends with someone who is always putting everything he knows into a magazine.

Everybody loves everybody again.

"Department stores . . . $40,000"

NOVEMBER 15, 1962 / We served as insulation tonight for a family squabble over finances at the White House. Jackie had just learned (remarkably enough) that her husband was giving his salary to charity,* and had told

* The day before, White House sources had revealed that Kennedy had been giving his salary to various charities since he entered Congress in 1947. His salary as president was $100,000. The charities were not identified at the time, but Dave Powers recently identified them as including: the Girl Scouts, the Boy Scouts, United Negro College Fund, Boys Club of America, National Association for Retarded Children, Girls Club of America, and Federation of Jewish Philanthropies.

him early that day that she sure could use the money herself. A series of questions had evidently ensued, which led to a request for information from the president about the state of the family finances. He had the information in a letter, which he had with him and which had him boiling . . . not so much mad, as amazed and indignant. The item that had him really bugged was "Department Stores . . . $40,000." No one had an explanation, much less Jackie. No furnishings for the White House, and as Jackie pointed out, "no sable coat, or anything." Kennedy announced that he had called in Carmine Bellino, an accounting expert for various Senate committees on deciphering the financial records of Mafiosi and a long-time Kennedy friend, to straighten out the family finances. He said Bobby had recently called in Bellino to straighten out Ethel's finances. They were so tangled, the president said, that Bellino had had to move into the Hickory Hill house to find out who was stealing what.

Kennedy said he could understand why running for the presidency was expensive. He had spent and spent, he said—all of it capital. But "once you're in here, this is a place where a fellow should at least break even, with all the services provided." He revealed that his valet, George Thomas, and Jackie's maid, Provie Paredes, had both been put on civil service. This Jackie denied, but the president, offering to bet her, said he knew because he had just approved a promotion for both.

The Cuban missile crisis had just ended as a Kennedy triumph, and he hadn't said a word to me about it until tonight. I asked how he was sure the Russians weren't taking out old telephone poles instead of missiles under those canvas covers that appeared on the decks of the Soviet ships in the intelligence pictures. Kennedy admitted they had never seen those missiles without the covers on, and they looked the same leaving Cuba as they had looked en route to Cuba. But he emphasized that it really made little difference. If the Soviets did not take the missiles out, this would become known sooner or later; and the Russians knew for sure that that would mean immediate and massive invasion of Cuba by the United States to get the missiles out. Certainly Castro had no interest in keeping offensive missiles there, Kennedy said, for he knew this just as well as Khrushchev. The president and the administration just assume, therefore, that the missiles are on their way out. They assume, he said, that no missiles are in the caves, at least no MRBMs or IRBMs. And this assumption is based primarily on the evidence he has of their removal plus their conviction that both Khrushchev and Castro know the U.S. will invade if *any* offensive missiles are found.

During dinner, Adlai Stevenson telephoned the president to report on a session he'd just had with Vasily Kuznetsov, the Soviet deputy foreign minister.* I couldn't smoke out any details of that session, but after hanging up, the president called McGeorge Bundy and set up a meeting of ExCom—the ad hoc group that had handled the Cuban missile crisis—to discuss the memorandum he'd just asked Stevenson to prepare, before sending Assistant Secretary of State George Ball up to New York. The president referred to Stevenson in a manner that did nothing to dispel the rumors that he was less than 100 percent behind his UN ambassador.

---

* This meeting, and presumably the memorandum, dealt with the warning sent that day by Castro to the effect that Cuba would shoot down any U.S. plane flying reconnaissance missions over Cuban territory. The immediate U.S. response was that the overflights would continue.

Jackie had her portable victrola going full tilt throughout the Kennedy-Stevenson telephone conversation.

Howard K. Smith, the TV commentator, had just surfaced Alger Hiss for a special ABC broadcast on "The Political Obituary of Richard M. Nixon" (!). Kennedy called it "a typical demonstration of phony liberals," and expressed concern that it might help Nixon, even though he feels that Nixon is "beyond saving," politically. He said he thinks Nixon is "sick."

Newsweek had Rockefeller on the cover this week, and the president thought the picture of Rocky was terrific. I told him Rockefeller had denied—again—the quote he had given us to the effect that he could have beaten Kennedy in 1960, and could beat him in 1964. "Nobody ever had any doubt he could beat me in 1960," the president said, implying that 1964 was something else again. "I knew that." Kennedy is now convinced that Rockefeller will be his opponent in 1964, and says he isn't sure that Barry Goldwater won't be on the ticket with him. As much as he liked the cover, he said he felt an even better cover would have been "Dad," his father, who now has one son as president, another as attorney general, and a third as a U.S. senator. I reminded him that we had wanted to put all three of "Dad's boys" on the cover, but he said we had blown the timing. Talking about his father, Kennedy revealed that he can now say only two words, "out" and "no," but he can apparently still understand what is said to him, and enjoys being talked to and clued into family activities and accomplishments.

The Kennedys had a picture of Adenauer holding little John in his arms, which had apparently been taken that day. Kennedy was filled with admiration for *Der Alte's* virility, if not his personality. He noted several times with wonder how Adenauer had thrown

John up into the air—all this at the age of eighty-six. Jackie couldn't resist what sounded like an unfair dig, given the condition of the president's back, saying that it was the first time anyone had ever thrown little John into the air. This brought up the subject of children, and Jackie went on at great length and with obvious pride about "John-John," how problem-free he was, how much he loved his father, and loved to be around him. She talked about Dino and Marina in glowing terms, especially Marina.

Back to Cuba . . . and an explosion by the president about his forceful, positive lack of admiration for the Joint Chiefs of Staff, except for Maxwell Taylor, whom he calls "absolutely first-class."

"The first advice I'm going to give my successor," the president said, "is to watch the generals and to avoid feeling that just because they are military men their opinions on military matters are worth a damn."

"They are always there with their pencils out"

NOVEMBER 27, 1962 / Jim Fosburgh dined at the White House this night with us and the Kennedys. He's president of Jackie's painting committee and married to Vincent Astor's former wife. He and Jackie told a fascinating story about a woman who had left six Cézannes to the U.S. government provided the paintings hung either in the American embassy in Paris, or in the White House. For years they had hung in neither, until Jackie heard about them on one of her prowls and asked to see them. Four of them are apparently inferior, and Jackie was first shown only these four by John Walker, head of the National Gallery. She spotted the other two behind burly guards and asked to see them. They were, of course, the two good ones, which Walker in an exercise of instinctive territorial imperative wanted to hold on to. They've been hanging in the White House for a few days.

Fosburgh also reported to Jackie that the employees of Sears, Roebuck had chipped in enough money to buy four paintings of American Indians for the White House. They are not by the famous Indian painter, Frederic Remington, but by someone even better, according to Fosburgh: Charles Bird King, and even rarer, since almost all his paintings are in Europe.

The president was in a good mood, though he seemed preoccupied at first, and the conversation jumped around as it invariably does. The Kennedys asked us if we had heard—and liked—the record "The First Family," in which Vaughn Meader does various skits in a truly remarkable imitation of Kennedy. The president said, with just a hint of condescension, that he thought parts of it were amusing: the "Good night, Jackie, good night, Bobby, good night, Ethel" skit, the press conference, and especially the imitation of him saying to Dirksen "Ev, you drive a hard bargain" ("haad baagain"). My favorite accent came in the phrase "The swan is mine" ("The sworn is mine"), and he smiled when I said so. Kennedy told an interesting story about the skit on the record, which has the "president" saying "Of course, I, as a Catholic, could never vote for him" about a possible Jewish president.

Apparently, Arthur Schlesinger heard this portion of the record on the radio driving to work, and only this portion. It occurred to him that millions of listeners might have mistaken the imitation for the real thing and assume that Kennedy was anti-Semitic. In describing his concern to the president, Schlesinger recalled that Franklin D. Roosevelt had had more imitators than any other American politician. Kennedy asked Schlesinger ("That was Arthur's assignment for the week," he said) to see what Roosevelt had done to prevent imitations from being broadcast. Schlesinger had just reported back. Apparently FDR's press secretary, Steve Early, had called all the White House reporters (about a dozen of them) into his office one morning in 1934, and told them, "It is the policy of the White House that no imitations of the president will be carried over the airwaves." We laughed for a while, thinking of the outcry that would ensue today if Salinger delivered a similar dictum to the White House press corps.

The president reflected several times about Cuba and Khrushchev, and what it feels like to go eyeball-to-eyeball. He was philosophical about it, but he said the inevitability of it all was so discouraging. And the stakes were too high for inevitability, where one false step, one simple misunderstanding, could wipe out "all of us at this table and our children." The question that really haunts him is why Khrushchev did not do what he said very clearly at Vienna that he was going to do . . . namely, liquidate Berlin. "He said it over and over and over again," Kennedy emphasized. "And why didn't he do it?" I reminded him that Llewellyn Thompson, former U.S. ambassador to Moscow and a key Kennedy advisor during the Cuban missile crisis, had expressed reservations at the time. "I know," the president said. "Tommy was one of those who predicted that Khrushchev would back down on Berlin." Tommy obviously stands high with the commander-in-chief.

We had seen Kennedy in Vienna during his talks with Khrushchev only in large crowds. For weeks after he returned he talkeed about little else, and he carried excerpts from the official translation of his talks with Khrushchev around with him wherever he went, and read chunks of them to me several times. In the first few meetings with the Soviet leader there were even a few cold war type jokes.

At lunch one day, Secretary of State Dean Rusk boasted to Khrushchev about a new kind of experimental American corn that grew three feet from seed in sixty days. Khrushchev interrupted Rusk by saying, "I know that's what you told Gromyko in Geneva, and he told me, but I wrote a friend of mine in America (this turned out to be Roswell Garst, whose Iowa farm Khrushchev had visited during his trip to the United States), and he told me it wasn't true." Later Khrushchev was boasting to Kennedy about Soviet feats, including a newly developed process of making vodka out of natural gas. Kennedy interrupted Khrushchev this time to tell him "That sounds like some of Dean Rusk's sixty-day corn to me." Khrushchev apparently roared with laughter, and told Rusk "Both of us are being attacked and we must defend ourselves." On the following day, at the lunch given by the Soviets, Kennedy asked Khrushchev about the two medals he was wearing. Khrushchev bent his pudgy chin down to his chest and started explaining: "This one is the Lenin Peace Prize," and before he could describe the second one, Kennedy turned to the translator and said "Tell him I hope they never take it away from him." Kennedy reported the Soviet leader had thought this was a thigh-slapper.

But all jocularity disappeared at the third Kennedy-Khrushchev session, requested by the president to nail down the Soviet position on Berlin. "This was the nut-cutter," Kennedy said more than once later. The president told Khrushchev it was not so much the Soviet determination to sign a separate peace treaty with East Germany that bothered him, as it was the Soviet interpretation that such a treaty would make West Berlin irrevocably East German. That was not acceptable to the United States. Acceptable or not, Khrushchev thundered back, it was going to happen—in December, six months later. "If the U.S. wants to go to war," Kennedy quoted Khrushchev slowly, "that's your business, but you must understand that force will be met with force."

Kennedy said he replied "It looks like a cold winter," and the two parted.

The president was interested in *Newsweek*'s difficulties with Arthur Sylvester, long-time Washington bureau chief of the *Newark Evening News,* turned assistant secretary of defense for public affairs, the fancy title for the Pentagon flack. "It's a tough job," Kennedy said, "but Sylvester obviously isn't the man for it. Salinger is perfect, the way he doesn't let anything get him down." Kennedy wanted to know each of the five misstatements of fact that Sylvester had charged *Newsweek* with. I listed them, and he didn't blink an eye—or deny it—when I came to the one in which Lloyd Norman *(Newsweek*'s Pentagon correspondent) had reported that there was some evidence that the range of the Soviet missiles in Cuba had been overestimated by the administration, intentionally or otherwise.

There was much discussion about *Newsweek,* as usual. He sops up newspaper gossip like a blotter. When will *Newsweek* go ahead of *Time,* he asked at one point. He applauded the end of what he had told Phil Graham was *Newsweek*'s "no win" policy of never knocking *Time.* He was highly critical of the Luce publications, noting with glee that he felt *Look* was much better than *Life,* and *Newsweek* was better than *Time,* and getting better.

Both he and Jackie wanted to know when "Eminent John" was going to work for us (Emmet John Hughes, a long-time Luce correspondent and Eisenhower aide, who had just been named *Newsweek* columnist), why Phil Graham had hired him, what I thought of him. "Of course, we all know and love Emmet," the president said. "He's a son of a bitch." As evidence, he offered only what he called a misquotation in an article Hughes had just written for *Look*, part of his second Eisenhower book, *The Ordeal of Power.* The book reminded him of the danger inherent in having historians work for any administration. (Kennedy had only one truly professional historian working in the White House. This was Schlesinger, whom he admired as a historian, liked enormously as a person, but whose liberal politics he felt were impractical.) "Those bastards," he proclaimed as if he were literally surrounded by active historians, "they are always there with their pencils out."

The president was determined to see a movie, even though Jackie said the choices were strictly limited. Jackie read off the list of what was available, and the president selected the one we had all unanimously voted against, a brutal, sadistic little Western called *Lonely Are The Brave*. Kennedy watched, lying down on a bed placed in the front row, his head propped up on pillows.

"When we don't have to go through you bastards"

DECEMBER 17, 1962 / The president went on television live tonight, answering questions from each network's White House correspondent—Sander Vanocur of NBC, Bill Lawrence of ABC (both friends of Kennedy), and George Herman of CBS.

I watched it at home, and felt professionally threatened as a man who was trying to make a living by the written word. The program was exceptionally good, well-paced, colorful, humorous, serious, and I felt that a written account would have paled by comparison. After it was over I called Kennedy to tell him all this.

"Well," he told me, "I always said that when we don't have to go through you bastards, we can really get our story over to the American people."

"Some pipeline I have into the White House"

JANUARY 30, 1963 / Douglas and Phyllis Dillon gave a dinner dance tonight, with the Kennedys as guests of honor. At one point in the evening I spotted the president and Teddy Kennedy standing together, with Teddy doing all the talking and the president roaring with laughter.

"Some pipeline I have into the White House," Teddy Kennedy said to me when I joined them. "I tell him 1,000 men are out of work in Fall River; 400 men out of work in Fitchburg. And when the Army gets that new rifle, there's another 600 men out of work in Springfield. And do you know what he says to me? 'Tough shit.'"

"17,000 Soviet troops in Cuba" and "27,000 U.S. troops in Turkey"

FEBRUARY 11, 1963 / We dined alone with the president last night. Jackie did not appear. We saw a dreadful movie about some Englishmen in a German prison camp, and then just before midnight walked around the Ellipse in the cold, pouring rain. Counting all the

Secret Service men, we made up a task force, but no one recognized the president.

Conversation before that had been relaxed but scattered. The physical fitness craze was in full swing, and Kennedy asked our advice about whether he should let Salinger go on his planned fifty-mile hike Friday. "We all know and love Plucky," he said about his jovial press secretary, "and we think he's funny. But I wonder what the rest of the country thinks of him. I wonder if they don't think he's making an ass out of himself." The implications were pretty clear, and thirty-six hours later, Salinger announced he was canceling his hike. This led Kennedy and me to a discussion of how far we thought we could make it on a hike, cold turkey, or as the president put it, "in our Peal shoes." He guessed he could go fifteen miles.

The question of official gifts from the United States to visiting dignitaries came up. Kennedy was appalled that the gift scheduled for King Moulay Hassan of Morocco was a regular hi-fi set, in a "French Provincial console." The president said he had overruled the gift and sent it back to the chief of protocol with a request that he come up with something more indigenously American and more special. He showed us the present that Jackie had personally designed for the King of Laos, who is coming to town in a few days. It was a jagged chunk of a brilliant green stone found in Arizona. It had been elaborately bound with a gold link chain, and was very striking.

Newsweek was planning another cover story on Bobby Kennedy, and as usual I asked the president for help. He told me two—shocking—stories that I'd never heard before. The first involved an official of the Teamsters Union, allegedly a pal of Teamsters chief Jimmy Hoffa, who had been convicted, sentenced, and then suddenly started to "sing." He was apparently beginning to tell all when he was suddenly taken ill and rushed to the hospital, where it was found that he was suffering from acute arsenic poisoning. The president said the Teamsters had apparently heard this man was squealing, and had quite simply tried to poison him. The second anecdote concerned the recent discovery by the Justice Department of some hoodlum who reported he had been hired by the Teamsters, given a gun fitted with a silencer, and sent to Washington with what the president said were orders to kill the attorney general. I found this one a little hard to believe, but the president was obviously serious. Kennedy said Bobby was anxious that the first story not get out, for fear that it would so terrify all potential anti-Hoffa Teamsters that the anti-Hoffa cause would be lost. Neither story ran in *Newsweek*.

After the movie, Kennedy took us on a tour. He showed us the new Blue Room, worrying that the blue of the curtains and the blue of the chairs added up to a bit too much. He showed us the new Green Room, which he liked very much, except for the Eisenhower portrait, which he had hung about as high as a painting can be hung. And then he led us over to his office to see his collection of scrimshaw, a new model ship he had just been given, and the holes in the floor left by President Eisenhower's golf shoes. From there we went to the newly decorated downstairs dining room, where he meets with the congressional leaders, and finally to the Cabinet Room. Kennedy told the story of the cabinet table, shaped like two elongated trapezoids joined together at their broad ends. He said the table had been the gift of Jesse Jones, FDR's secretary of commerce, and designed by him, because it was the only design which permitted Jones, who was deaf, to see and read the lips of everyone at the table, no matter where he sat.

We talked a lot about Cuba. The president said that the presence of 17,000 Soviet troops in Cuba, ninety miles from the U.S., was one thing viewed by itself, but it was something else again when you knew there were 27,000 U.S. troops stationed in Turkey, right on the Soviet border, and they had been there some years. He warned me against releasing this information. Obviously, it is classified, and just as obviously it would be politically suicidal for him publicly to equate the two. "It isn't wise politically to understand Khrushchev's problems in quite this way," he said, quietly.

"What the hell do we need those for?"

FEBRUARY 12, 1963 / Jackie was back in circulation tonight at dinner, with Eve and Harry Labouisse and Nancy and Teddy White, whose book *The Making of the President, 1960* had benefited enormously from his friendship with Kennedy and from Kennedy's pre-occupation with historians.

Cuba was much discussed again, with the president again talking about the 27,000 U.S. troops in Turkey. He seems almost to believe the case that Khrushchev can make for keeping 17,000 troops close to our borders, as long as we keep 27,000 troops on his borders. Labouisse talked quietly and intermittently about Greece, where he is the U.S. ambassador. He outlined problems he foresaw in connection with construction of a NATO missile range on the island of Crete. No matter who ran the base or built it, he said, the Americans were going to get blamed for it, and before he could even ask the president to intervene, JFK whipped out a pencil and a piece of paper, and said "What the hell do we need those missiles for, anyway?" He was obviously writing a note to himself. He relished Labouisse's report of getting a copy of the recent Kennedy interview with network correspondents, having it translated and distributed to Greek theaters. The prime minister's wife had apparently asked for a copy of it and shown it to a group of women . . . and all the time Kennedy nodded delightedly.

There was discussion of David Schoenbrun's problems. Schoenbrun was part of the original team of radio and TV foreign correspondents put together by Edward R. Murrow for CBS. Schoenbrun had come close to owning Paris as a journalist when Labouisse and I were in the embassy there in the mid-fifties, but he had run into a lot of trouble since being named Washington bureau chief of CBS in January, 1962, to succeed Howard K. Smith. Anyone who knows David loves and admires him, first, then launches into a series of anecdotes about how difficult and self-important he can be. Labouisse and I ran through a few of our favorite Schoenbrun stories, and Kennedy said he saw how difficult he could be, but said that Schoenbrun had seemed to him to be articulate and intelligent on the few occasions their paths had crossed.

Stuart Symington's name came up, with all agreeing what a nice guy he is. Kennedy repeated what he has often said . . . that he felt that if he had been stopped at the Los Angeles convention, the delegates would have eventually picked Symington.

CONVERSATIONS WITH KENNEDY

Kennedy brought up Richard Nixon's name, and said without vindictiveness that he felt the country was lucky that Nixon had not been president during the Cuban missile crisis.

UPI PHOTO

Kennedy confers with Nixon over the Cuban missile crisis. "Kennedy brought up Richard Nixon's name, and said without vindictiveness that he felt the country was lucky that Nixon had not been president during the Cuban missile crisis."

"You can't beat brains"

FEBRUARY 20, 1963 / As usual, the president wanted
to know *Newsweek*'s cover, and when I told him at
dinner it was Mac Bundy, and asked him for an on-
the-record assessment, he said simply "You can't beat
brains," and told us how impressed he had been recently with Ted Sorensen's knowledge about the aged and
the problems of aging during a discussion that afternoon. The value to me and to *Newsweek* of these
presidential asides is enormous. It not only gives me
a good understanding of who's riding high in presidential esteem, but it gives me early warning of subjects occupying the president's attention. Tomorrow
morning, I will alert *Newsweek* to the fact that aging
and the aged have been the subject of recent high-
level White House meetings, and I suspect we will
crank up our own inquiry. "Bundy gets the work done,"
Kennedy went on. "He does just a tremendous amount
of work. And he's got a damn good staff down there."
He mentioned Carl Kaysen, one of Bundy's top as-
sistants (now head of Princeton's Institute of Advanced
Study), and said Kaysen couldn't articulate as well as
Bundy "but he wrote the best memo I ever saw on the
multi-national force." Kennedy said he particularly
admired Bundy's ability to shrug off criticism and to
remain unflustered. The multi-national force reference
prompted me to ask him how seriously the U.S. wanted
such a force. Kennedy came back with the quick

"what" which is so typical when he is asked about something he hasn't clearly decided in his own mind. He gave an evasive answer which translated meant to me that he was not terribly serious about it.

At dinner, the conversation turned, as usual, to the subject of reporters, and specifically to the subject of which reporter was "the biggest S.O.B." Kennedy warmed to the subject, to put it mildly, and in a matter of a few seconds had awarded first prize to Dick Wilson, the veteran Washington bureau chief of the Cowles newspapers and a syndicated columnist. "He's a Charlie-Uncle-Nan-Tare," the president said bluntly, as he got up to take off his coat at dinner. (But a few months later, Dick Wilson wrote a column about the Kennedy family, and particularly about how Kennedy was a fine family man. That changed the president's mind, pronto. "Good man, that Wilson," he told us with a smile. "Great columnist. Sincere.") Jackie's question, "What is a Charlie-Uncle-Nan-Tare, for heaven's sake?" went unanswered. (Kennedy's earthy language was a direct result of his experience in the service, as it was for so many men of his generation, whose first serious job was war. Often it had direct Navy roots, as above when he used the signalman's alphabet. He used "prick" and "fuck" and "nuts" and "bastard" and "son of a bitch" with an ease and comfort that belied his upbringing, and somehow it never seemed offensive, or at least it never seemed offensive to me.) Other candidates for the biggest S.O.B. in journalism to get a call from the president of the United States included Roscoe Drummond, the former *Christian Science Monitor* bureau chief, now a columnist for the *New York Herald Tribune;* Lyle Wilson, chief of the Washington bureau of United Press; Earl Mazo of the *Herald Tribune* (a friend and sometime ghost writer of Richard Nixon); and Arthur Krock, the distinguished Pulitzer Prize-winning Washington correspondent of the *New York Times,* once a firm Kennedy family friend, who had written the introduction to Kennedy's college thesis later published as the book *Why England Slept.* Kennedy told me that Krock had never forgiven him for the *Newsweek* story on the Washington press corps, in which I had quoted the president as saying that he no longer read Krock. Dave Kraslow, then of the *Herald Tribune,* and Bill McGaffin, of the *Chicago Daily News,* were cited by the president as reporters who were consistently ornery at press conferences.

During dinner Kennedy tried to sell me on a "lead article" about how things were really not as bad for the United States as they might seem after a series of small "slippages." In fact, the president said, "Things are in pretty good shape. If what had happened to the Russians in the last few months had happened to the United States, they'd be trying to impeach us, and they'd be right. The people forget that." And he listed some of the reverses the Soviets had suffered recently: withdrawal of the missiles from Cuba, of course; Albania had been overtly critical of Khrushchev's policies during the Cuban missile crisis; so had Red China; the rift between Russia and China was growing wider; a Soviet trade mission had just left Shanghai in a huff; and a series of "economic crime" trials inside the Soviet Union had led to at least twelve death sentences and more than a hundred jail sentences.

Kennedy brought up some recent experiences—right out of Kafka—with his father. Apparently, the old man's health is deteriorating. All he can say now is "no." The president says his phone rings regularly, and it's Ann Gargan, saying that the ambassador wants to talk. Kennedy says he grits his teeth and rattles on, while the voice on the other end of the telephone says "no, no, no."

The date of the next White House dance has been set for March 8. "We've got to have them in honor of somebody, so we've chosen Gene Black (Eugene Black, director of the World Bank)," Jackie reported. "The only trouble is that now he keeps calling up every five minutes and wants some aunt or friend to be asked."

At about 9:15 the president got up and went to the Oval Room, where a group of senators and their wives had been waiting to join the president at a movie . . . including the Edmondsons of Oklahoma, the Bayhs of Indiana, the Nelsons from Wisconsin, the McIntires from New Hampshire, Gale McGee from Wyoming, and Ed Muskie of Maine. The Kennedys had been congratulating themselves throughout dinner on this new form of entertainment. "We only have to spend about fifteen minutes of our time," Jackie said, "and they obviously have an enjoyable evening." We saw *The Ugly American,* but the president was called out fifteen minutes after the movie started. It was Mac Bundy, we learned later, calling with the news that two Cuban MIGs had strafed an American shrimp boat about sixty miles north of Havana.*

When the movie was over and the senators had left, the Kennedys asked us back upstairs for a nightcap. Jackie put some records on ("Alley Cat," and bossa

---

* The boat, *Ala,* had been adrift for three days because of engine trouble, and its crew was unhurt. U.S. jet interceptors were scrambled when the MIGs were spotted by radar on Key West, and the MIGs turned tail when the American jets approached. In response to a U.S. letter of protest, the Cubans denied shooting at the boat, said they had only buzzed it.

novas), and the telephone rang. Bundy again. At one point I heard Kennedy ask "Were they Negroes?" and later I asked him why that question. Two of the crewmen were named Washington and Jackson, he replied.

"I sure was mad, but I forget why now"

FEBRUARY 27, 1963 / Jackie was in Palm Beach last night when we dined with Kennedy alone, and first crack out of the barrel he was talking about Phil Graham and his efforts to settle the printers' strike that had closed down New York newspapers. Phil had called him off and on all Saturday afternoon in Palm Beach, the president said. He apparently let Andy Hatcher (Andrew Hatcher, the assistant White House press secretary) handle the calls for a few hours, and then when he tried a fifth time through Evelyn Lincoln, the president's private secretary, the president took the call. Graham reported that he had just spent six hours with Bert Powers, head of the New York printers' union, Kennedy said. Graham told the president that Powers was right, that Kennedy had been seriously misinformed when he attacked Powers at his last press conference. Graham asked the president to issue a statement saying that he had been misinformed. Kennedy said he asked Phil if Powers were present as he was telephoning. Graham said that he was, and apparently asked Powers to leave the room—loudly, so Kennedy could plainly overhear. The president said he told Graham that Powers didn't have to leave the room, that he was not going to discuss the matter, and that he was certainly not going to issue any statement that he had been misinformed. The conversation lasted only a few minutes, and when it was over, Kennedy said he asked someone to contact Ted Kheel, Mayor John Lindsay's labor expert, and get him to "call Graham off."

Holding his thumb and forefinger close together, the president said "The line is so damn narrow between rationality and irrationality in Phil."

(In fact, Phil Graham was seriously ill, in and out of debilitating depressions between periods of erratic, often brilliant activity. He was to die by his own hand in less than six months. When he was well, he was one of the most naturally attractive, witty, and brilliant men I've ever known—and a natural friend for Kennedy, as JFK was a natural friend for Graham. They shared humor, understanding of the uses and abuses of power, charm, common goals for America, and much more. The strain that Graham's illness was putting on their friendship, and Kennedy's loyalty to him and to his wife, was sad and moving.)

Tony asked the president how come he had left classified documents with Graham at the Carlyle Hotel some weeks before, as Graham had been telling friends. Kennedy said that the briefcase he had left with Phil, regardless of how Phil might have described it, was hardly a briefcase of "national crises." Instead, he described it as a "bunch of documents" guessing what de Gaulle might be up to. It did include a cable from Douglas MacArthur in Brussels (the general's nephew, now U.S. ambassador to Belgium), Kennedy admitted, and presumably this cable must have been classified. But Kennedy said "He has been good to me and good to this country, and I want to help him out."

Talk of Graham led us to a broad discussion of the power of the press, which fascinated the president, as the use and abuse of all power fascinated him. He cited *Newsweek*'s handling of the Blauvelt case, which he said had reduced White House mail on the subject from 500 letters a week to zero in seven days. Tony interrupted him at this point to remind him "You were so mad at Ben when he went up to Newport to write that story." The president laughed, and said "I sure was mad at him, but I forget why, now."

I reminded him that the straw that had broken the camel's back had been the *Look* piece by Fletcher Knebel. Kennedy got all excited again, this time without anger, and said, "I remember. Why the hell didn't you deny it the next day to the *Herald Tribune,* instead of giving us all that jazz about how your former editor (Denson) would tuck it to you if you said anything more? It didn't make any difference if you said it or not. All you had to do was tell Donovan you didn't." I took advantage of this opening to tuck it to my friend —and competitor—Hugh Sidey of *Time* magazine: "I know, the way Sidey told the *Herald Tribune* how wonderful all you Kennedys are to the press, and then Sidey tucks it to you every week."

Kennedy anger was an impermanent emotion, even though he could get good and mad on occasion, as he did with the steel magnates when they raised prices. He once told me the only time he truly lost his temper at the White House was at Barbara Gamarekian, one of the secretaries in Pierre Salinger's press office. She used to come into the president's secretary's office to raid an ice box hidden there, and this bugged the president. He caught her doing it once more than he could stand, and blew up. "I took an inch and a half off her head," he said, "and I shouldn't have done it."

I told him about Arthur Krock's column yesterday which seemed to me to be saying that managed news was news given any reporter except Krock. Kennedy said he had not read the column, but when I told him Ken Crawford was going after Krock by name in his *Newsweek* column this week, he said, "Tell Ken to bust it off in old Arthur. He can't take it, and when you go after him he folds."

Mention of Sidey reminded the president of a story Romulo Betancourt, president of Venezuela, had told him when they had met recently. It seems Betancourt had told Kennedy how able the *Time* correspondents in Latin America were. "The trouble is," Kennedy quoted Betancourt as saying, "their reporters file the Bible to New York, and the magazine prints the Koran."

Kennedy said he liked the Bundy cover, and told us a story I could have used in my Bundy file. Professor Charles R. Cherington, whom *Newsweek* had described as critical of Bundy when Mac was dean of the faculty of arts and science at Harvard and Cherington was teaching government in 1953, apparently referred to Bundy as a "son of a bitch" in one of his classes. In his next lecture, Cherington told his students that one of them had apparently reported this description to Bundy, who had then summoned Cherington to his office. There, Cherington told his class, he had apologized to Bundy for calling him a son of a bitch, and Bundy had apologized to him for being one. The president said the *Newsweek* cover story had produced one "medium-sized flap" inside the administration. *Newsweek* had said that Bundy had once resolved a dispute between the Central Intelligence Agency and the Strategic Air Command, a dispute which had prevented air reconnaissance of Cuba for a period of two weeks. The story was wrong, the president said, but he wouldn't say whether it was wrong because Bundy had not resolved the dispute, or wrong because the dispute had not prevented photo-reconnaissance. "I don't have the details," he said. "I just know it was wrong."

I told Kennedy that *France-Soir* was coming out with a story tomorrow saying that the head of the anti-de Gaulle pro-French Algeria forces, who had recently been arrested in France, had recently been in touch with the CIA here. That story was false, the president said, and had been proved to be false. He told of having called in George Ball and Dean Rusk and asking them to do something about it. He said they'd told him Bill Tyler (William Royall Tyler, the assistant secretary of state for European affairs) was sending a cable to Chip Bohlen (Charles E. Bohlen, long-time U.S. Soviet expert, now ambassador to France). The president said he had blown his stack, and called Tyler on the telephone in Rusk's and Ball's presence. "What the hell good is a fucking cable," he quoted himself as asking Tyler. "What are you saving, thirty dollars? Call Chip on the telephone, and get him to see what he can do about killing the story." The president was appalled that Tyler, experienced as he was, would handle an urgent problem that way.

From last week's cover on Bundy, it was only a step to next week's cover—Bobby Kennedy again. I asked the president why he thought Bobby was great . . . "and never mind the brother bit." Here is his answer:

"First, his high moral standards, strict personal ethics. He's a puritan, absolutely incorruptible. Then he has this terrific executive energy. We've got more guys around here with ideas. The problem is to get things done. Bobby's the best organizer I've ever seen. Even in touch football, four or five guys on a team, it was always Bobby's team that won, because he had it organized the best, the best plays. He's got compassion, a real sense of compassion. Those Cuban prisoners (from the Bay of Pigs episode) weighed on his mind for eighteen months. And it's got nothing to do with publicity or politics. In Palm Beach now, I bet there isn't one of the (Cuban exile) leaders who hasn't been invited to his house to be with his family. His loyalty comes next. It wasn't the easiest thing for him to go to (Joe) McCarthy's funeral. (No explanation of why it wasn't the easiest thing: namely, that JFK was running for president, and taking real heat for having been soft on McCarthy.) And then when Jean McCarthy's new husband needed a job, Bobby got him appointed to something."*

We went late to a movie, *The Seven Deadly Sins.*

"He's going to do a helluva business"

MARCH 6, 1963 / We spent a lot of time at dinner tonight, alone with the Kennedys, talking about our children. Tony had been over at the White House with all the children except Marina since 3 o'clock. They had played outside, seen a movie, and visited the president's office with Evelyn Lincoln. Little John had left the movie suddenly, quickly followed by Dino. Subsequent reports are confused, but Dino reports that

---

* G. Joseph Minetti, appointed to the Civil Aeronautics Board in 1962, was married to Senator Joseph McCarthy's widow.

John clobbered him with a chair. Dino was more upset by a dead bird the children had found somewhere than by his wounds. He says he loves Caroline, but unfortunately Caroline loves Nancy. Kennedy was complimentary to Tony about our children, especially Dino. "My God, he's a good looking child," he said. "Those eyes. He's going to do a helluva business." We had a long conversation at dinner about what ages we would like to be now, if we could change our ages. (Kennedy was forty-six, Jackie was thirty-two, Tony was thirty-nine, and I was forty-two.) The president stated he would like to change places with Dino, specifically not with his son, John. We all jumped on that, doubting it vocally, but he repeated it "except for the fact that I'm president now." Jackie said she thought the ages from eight to eighteen were "useless."

I brought up the subject of how hard I'd found it to get Bobby Kennedy right in the *Newsweek* cover story. It is so hard to answer the question "What's he like?" about anyone interesting, with all the contradictions in all of us. "That's what makes journalism so fascinating," the president commented, "and biography so interesting . . . the struggle to answer the single question, 'What's he like?' " I said I thought Bobby was full of contradictions—contradictions that made him tough to read but interesting to know. "I don't see any contradictions at all in Bobby," the president said bluntly. Jackie disagreed with him, saying "Oh, yes there are." She told a story about how Bobby had been the first one to come to her to help when she had lost her first baby. She stumbled, we thought quite uncomfortably, over JFK's absence, and said quickly "We couldn't get hold of Jack in time."

The president had held a press conference that morning, the first A.M. conference in months. He said he

thought "it didn't have a zip," and blamed himself.
The conference had started off with a tough question:
"Were the four dead fliers in fact working for CIA
when they were killed?" Kennedy's answer had been
convoluted and involved.* "What the hell am I going
to tell them?" he asked defensively, "that they did work
for the CIA? Why don't you write a story about how
many people have been killed working for the CIA?
There's a hell of a lot, I can tell you that." I said
Newsweek would like nothing more than to write such
a story, but wondered whether he had any reason to
believe that anyone would help provide the information.
His smile told me that *he* wouldn't.

Kennedy had gotten a big laugh from the reporters
in refusing to answer Marvin Kalb's question about his
views on the decade since Stalin's death, saying instead
that the decade was more properly the subject for a
half-hour special, which CBS had in fact scheduled
for that very evening. Kennedy swore that he had not
been aware of the special or the time, but he laughed
when I told him everyone assumed he had been so well
briefed that he knew Kalb, who had just arrived in
Washington for CBS, had done that particular show on
that particular subject for this particular night.

Kennedy reported that Phil Graham had apparently
written, for publication in the *Post,* an attack on Comsat, the private communications satellite agency. Kennedy had appointed Graham to Comsat's board of direc-
tors, and the article apparently said it was screwed up
and badly run. Kennedy revealed that he had persuaded

---

* Ten days earlier, Senator Mansfield had confirmed that
four civilian airmen from Alabama, part of a U.S. group train-
ing Cuban rebels, were killed during the 1961 Cuban invasion.
Although presumably part of the CIA operation, they were
never so identified.

Clark Clifford, the distinguished Washington lawyer who had counseled presidents since 1946, to involve himself and try to get the story pulled back. Clifford had done so.

Just before he left, the conversation jumped quickly from subject to subject, as if the president wanted to get through an agenda before quitting. This scatter-shot conversation was invariably a sure sign that the evening was winding down fast. Tonight's last-minute miscellany included:

—Why none of us had women friends with large bosoms. (No answers.)

—How Barry Goldwater (the senator from Arizona who was going to end up as the Republican candidate for president in 1964) was a nicer, more attractive man than Rockefeller (who then appeared to be the likelier GOP candidate).

—How Bobby might run for president some day, "but certainly not in 1968."

"Sometimes you have to eat it"

MARCH 12, 1963 / This was the first time we had seen the Kennedys since the dance last Friday, and the ritual rehash took much of our time. Jackie complained that the Eugene Blacks had not really understood they were only the "beards" for the party . . . that the Kennedys wanted to give a party, didn't dare give one for themselves, and so had selected the Blacks, as they had earlier selected the Gavins (Ambassador to France and

Mrs. James Gavin) to make the party more publicly acceptable. The Blacks had apparently asked to have so many of their friends invited, Jackie said, and that several Kennedy friends had to be uninvited, including old pals like Bill Walton and Mary Meyer.

We had again been part of the "in" crowd—we kept telling ourselves—that got asked to come after dinner at the White House again. We had met the Kennedys in the upstairs hall, and Jackie had greeted my wife bluntly, saying "Oh, Tony, you look terrific. My bust is bigger than yours, but then so is my waist." The females imported from New York for the occasion had been spectacular again, and at one point Kennedy had pulled me to one side to comment "If you and I could only run wild, Benjy."

Jackie reported that Betty Beale, the society columnist for the *Washington Star*, had learned about the party —as had anyone with the slightest interest in this kind of stuff—including a rumor that Godfrey McHugh's girl friend (he was the president's Air Force aide) had taken a dip in the pool at midnight, and had been seen later jumping on the bed in the Lincoln Room. Interestingly, Kennedy didn't question the rumor, but told Jackie to "get after McHugh." Jackie asked whether she should write him or call him, and was told "Call him tomorrow." Kennedy revealed that for the first time, they had someone specially assigned to count the booze. Apparently at an earlier dance the Kennedys had been charged for ninety bottles of assorted spirits and were convinced that they were being stolen blind. They were evidently correct, the president reported, for this time some hundred guests had consumed only thirty-three bottles of champagne and six bottles of the harder stuff.

The guest list at these parties is truly fascinating, for

it rarely, if ever, includes members of the Irish Mafia, the Irish Catholic political associates, generally from Boston, who are in many ways closer to Kennedy, personally as well as professionally, than the swingers or the intellectuals or the reporters. This is part of the fundamental dichotomy in Kennedy's character: half the "mick" politician, tough, earthy, bawdy, sentimental, and half the bright, graceful, intellectual *Playboy of the Western World;* and there aren't many people who cross over the dividing line. I suspect, outside his family, Kennedy is as comfortable with Larry O'Brien, Kenny O'Donnell, and Dave Powers as anyone else, but they are rarely mixed with the WASPs. One group feeds off the early, bachelor, political Kennedy, while the other group reflects the later, married, presidential Kennedy.

Jackie regaled us with reports of "two ghastly hours" she had spent earlier that day with three other mothers on duty as teachers' aides in Caroline's school. She could hardly wait to tell us about the adult games which the other mothers told her they played at their parties. One particular favorite, which Jackie illustrated, involved the males, tying a spoon to their waists so that it hung from their behinds down to a few inches above the floor, and then trying to extinguish a lighted candle with the broad end of the spoon. It was apparently the gyration, plainly obscene, that made it such "fun." The women would apparently stand on upside-down Old Fashioned glasses, and try something that would make them fall to the accompaniment of great laughter.

Out of the blue, Kennedy asked me if it was true that *Newsweek* was going to be sold. His question stunned me so that I gave what sounded like a wooden denial. *Newsweek* had been bought only two years ago, by Phil Graham and the *Washington Post*. When I asked him what he meant, the president said he had heard that five editors and executives of *Newsweek* had gone to Puerto Rico recently to tell Graham they had heard that Kay Graham and her family wanted to sell the magazine. He had few details, and when I told him that the editors had planned to go to Puerto Rico recently for some top-level editorial meeting, he quickly accepted that the rumors of a sale were false. I asked him to check his sources urgently and let me know, for I had been involved in one sale of *Newsweek* and wasn't up for another one. He told me to call Evelyn Lincoln in the morning.

We asked the president about his $1,000 bet with Chuck Spalding and Stash Radziwill, the Polish prince who was married to Jackie's sister Lee, that they couldn't complete the fifty-mile hike, which was still occasionally surfacing as a test of commitment to the New Frontier. Spalding was a born and practicing athlete, but Radziwill looked as if he hadn't seen a locker room for thirty years. Anyway, both of them made it, and the president had donated $1,000 to some charity (which he would not identify), according to the terms of the bet. They'd left at two in the morning, Kennedy revealed, and "with Stash, it was purely and simply a question of mind over matter." This led Kennedy to a discussion of pain generally. He asked Jackie and Tony, with a detached, almost clinical, interest, about how much pain was involved in childbirth. He contrasted their description of that pain with the pain he said he felt at that minute in his back. He said he thought he could stand any kind and any amount of pain, provided he knew that it would end.

Kennedy is scheduled to speak to the Washington conference of the Advertising Council tomorrow, and I asked him what he was going to tell them. "I don't know," he said, "and I don't know how much difference it makes. Sometimes I think I'm speaking to the same people over and over again, no matter which group of businessmen I'm talking to. Sidney Weinberg (the investment banker), my God, Roger Blough (head of U.S. Steel) . . . those people, I'm always talking to them."

Teddy Kennedy had recently been involved in some incident where he apparently jostled or roughed up a photographer from the Manchester, N.H., *Union-Leader,* the super-right-wing (and anti-Kennedy) newspaper owned by the strange iconoclast, William Loeb. Loeb had fired me once, when he bought the paper I had started on, and his editor was a onetime friend and colleague who now relished taking shots at me in his editorials, and so I voiced regret that Teddy had found it necessary to apologize. "Sometimes you have to eat it," the president said philosophically, "and this was one of them. If Teddy hadn't apologized, they would have tried to screw him when he runs again." Kennedy revealed that both Ted Sorensen and Clark Clifford had been involved in drafting Teddy's letter of apology. (Time and again, Clifford turns up to handle Kennedy family problems.) The president quoted Teddy as saying he was annoyed because "without that I'd have had a helluva free month."

In the last-minute miscellany department, the president made these observations:

—President Joao Goulart of Brazil, he had been told, had had his wife's lover taken out and shot to death.

—He referred to *Time*'s cover story on Chicago's Mayor Daley, and I asked him if he remembered what he had told us Daley said to him the night his election was hanging in the balance, about how "with a little bit of luck and the help of a few close friends," Illinois was safe. Kennedy had forgotten the story, apparently, but he laughed and said "Be sure to write that down."

—He asked me to tell Ken Crawford that he was disappointed Ken had changed "pompous" to "imperious" in his column on Arthur Krock.

As we got up to leave, Kennedy asked us all into his bedroom to see the ceramic jewelry box Tony had made him for Christmas. Without the slightest embarrassment he started undressing—shoes, socks, pants, and was unbuttoning his shirt, when I remarked that he had put on a little weight. Few things interest him more than a discussion of his own weight. "Isn't it fantastic?" he asked. "Friday I weighed 171, and everyone told me I was looking great. Four days later, I weigh 177 and I had two helpings of that dessert tonight (whipped cream, meringue and chocolate sauce)." I bet him he weighed more than 177 right now, and he rushed to the scales, but that's exactly what he did weigh. "But I weighed 175 after swimming," he bemoaned.

Kiss-and-tell journalism

MARCH 21, 1963 / Kennedy had just returned from Costa Rica, and the president's enthusiasm for the trip still sparkled when we saw them for dinner alone at the White House. His reception had been fantastic, he said, and he explained it by his youth, by the fact that he was a Democrat and a Catholic, and by Jackie's known ability to speak Spanish, even though she had not made this trip. He said he felt his inaugural address, letting the world know that the torch had passed to a new generation, meant more to Latin Americans than to anyone else. I asked him why he thought Nixon's trip to Latin America had failed. The visit was badly prepared, Kennedy answered—"Nixon represented the wrong party in FDR terms, and anyway Nixon is Nixon."

Tonight, after much prodding from Tony and pretty much to everyone's relief, I told the president for the first time that I was keeping a kind of diary of the times we met or talked. I got my opening when the conversation at dinner turned to Emmet Hughes' books on Eisenhower, *The Ordeal of Power,* which was being criticized as kiss-and-tell journalism. I was convinced he knew I was keeping some kind of record, and obviously did not object. I was not so sure about Jackie, who is much more nervous and easily distraught by this kind of thing. I told him that Tony had made me worry about not telling him, especially whenever the subject came up of those "bastard" historians who "are always there with their pencils out." I told him I certainly would not write anything about him as long as he was alive without his permission. Kennedy said there was no reason to wait that long. He insisted that he was glad that someone was keeping some kind of a record of the more intimate details without which the real story of any administration cannot be told. I am not convinced he knows how intimate those details might get, but I suspect Jackie does, but that's for another decade. Anyway, we agreed that I would not publish anything about our association with them without his permission for at least five years after they left the White House.

We talked next about their new house under construction outside Middleburgh on some rolling land which had been owned by Mr. and Mrs. Hubert B. Phipps. We ran a sketch of the plans in *Newsweek* last week, but Jack is plainly not on fire with the whole idea. They, especially the president, are worried about the cost. We have a complicated bet of a hundred dollars on how much it ends up costing. I say $75,000 and he says $50,000, and whoever is closer wins. Kennedy admitted tonight that the final figure would probably be $60,000, not $50,000. (It eventually cost more than $100,000 exclusive of land, and was sold by Jackie in 1964 for $225,000 including the land.)

At least once a night, our conversation turns to the news business, and tonight we zeroed in on news management, what it might be, and how much the president resents the charge that his administration is managing the news—as every administration has tried to do since George Washington. "It's a goddamn outrage," the president said, "when the *Washington Star* gives five times as much space to the TFX hearings where there is no funny business, than it does to the stockpile hearings, where old Stu (Symington) caught George Humphrey with his hand in the government till to the tune of a million dollars." A little simplistic, I thought; the problem is more sophisticated than that, but it was an interesting point.

"He'll carry me before I carry him"

MARCH 26, 1963 / We picked up where we left off yesterday on the subject of managed news at dinner alone with the Kennedys tonight. The president doesn't understand what people are talking about when they accuse him of managing the news. "You bastards are getting more information out of the White House—the kind of information you want when you want it—than ever before," he said. "Except for the Cuba thing, I challenge you to give me an example of our managing the news." I felt I was a potential example, but it seemed almost impolite to bring it up—especially after the flap caused by the Knebel piece. The president says the people who are charging him with managing the news are the people who aren't getting as much news as some others. I feel very comfortable right now in that second category, and will not look this gift horse in the mouth.

The president revealed that his special security committee had declared that the *New York Times*' military correspondent, Hanson Baldwin, in some article that Kennedy wouldn't identify, had committed a "major security violation." That had led to a "massive FBI investigation," Kennedy said, and that in turn had led to Baldwin's disenchantment.

(Kennedy rarely used the cloak of national security to disguise his displeasure at certain matters he wished he had not seen in print. This art form, brought to near perfection by the Nixon administration, is tough for journalists to handle. The American public, quite naturally, tends to believe a president or one of his high aides whenever he claims that national security requires that certain matters stay secret, and tends to be suspicious, to understate it, of claims by journalists that national security is not involved. But once Kennedy raised hell with me—in private—and even more private hell with the Pentagon, over a story *Newsweek* wanted to write about a new weapon being developed for Vietnam.

Lloyd Norman, *Newsweek*'s vacuum-cleaner Pentagon correspondent, returned to the office late one afternoon with a pocket full of small, blue plastic flechettes, each about the length of a paper clip. The body of these flechettes was about the diameter of a slim cigarette, sharply pointed at one end, with three or four fluted fins at the other end, like a miniature missile. Norman showed me a bunch of them, describing them as the latest weapon under development in Vietnam. Apparently they were designed to be dropped in a bomb, or artillery shell, fused to go off a few inches from the ground. When they exploded, hundreds of these deadly arrows would fly out in all directions, piercing whatever they met. Neither Norman or myself had ever seen or heard anything about flechettes, and I wondered how he had been able to get hold of them. He told me that "some colonel in the Pentagon had a drawer full of them," and simply gave him some. We were dining with the Kennedys that night and I asked Norman if he would let me have a couple to show the president—to show him what kind of information was volunteered to journalists, information to which I had no idea whether we had any legitimate title. I showed them to him during the course of the evening, and he was fascinated at first, then appalled. "You mean some dumb son of a bitch just handed these things to you?" I assured him that such was my information. Suddenly, he shot out of his chair, with the flechettes in his hand. "Bob McNamara is in the other room with Mac Bundy," he said, "and I'm going to show them to him and find out what the hell is going on."

A few minutes later he was back. "McNamara tells me those are as secret as anything going on in the Pentagon," the president reported, "and he's going to find out who the hell is passing them around."

Newsweek made a small Periscope item, some weeks later, about the development of a new plastic arrow as an anti-personnel weapon for use in jungle warfare, and Lloyd Norman was investigated from hell to breakfast. I always thought it was this incident that led to Norman's inclusion in the list of reporters "Jumped on by Jack" in Fletcher Knebel's piece in *Look* magazine about Kennedy and the press.)

The McClellan TFX hearings were much on his mind,* especially the report leaked a few days earlier that Secretary of Defense Bob McNamara had burst into tears in an executive session of the committee hearings, describing how his son Craig had asked him "Dad, when are they going to let you prove you're an honest man?" McNamara used those words, but denied

---

* The Senate Permanent Investigations Subcommittee began closed-door hearings Feb. 26, 1963 to investigate allegations of favoritism in the award the previous November of the contract for the TFX multipurpose combat plane to General Dynamics Corp., instead of Boeing Corp. Top Air Force and Navy officials, plus a 235-man evaluation team, favored Boeing's design, but they were overruled four times by McNamara, Air Force Secretary Eugene Zuckert, and Navy Secretary Fred Korth, who all favored General Dynamics. Although the hearings lasted most of the winter, no conflict of interest was established.

that he had wept. Kennedy said he had been so concerned about this leaked report that he had Carmine Bellino call Jerome S. Adlerman, the McClellan committee chief counsel, and ask for the details. The president had let Senator McClellan know he was threatening to issue a statement. Bellino reported back that McClellan had declined to comment when asked about the reports of McNamara's tears by a reporter. The senator told Bellino, Kennedy said, that he didn't mean by his "No comment" to say that McNamara had or had not cried. He just didn't see it, and maybe others did. This annoyed Kennedy even more, and led him to a discussion of senators generally and this committee in particular. "There's only one senator in the whole Senate that I don't see (understand)," the president said. "And that's Carl Curtis (the GOP senator from Nebraska). I can see Mundt (Karl Mundt, the South Dakota senator, known to the press gallery as "The Leaning Tower of Putty"), but I can't see Curtis. He can't talk; he's unprepossessing, and he's generally a shit." (These blunt characterizations of people in high places, earthy language and all, were invariably made casually, without venom, and seemingly with complete understanding that those so characterized felt the same way about him.)

King Hassan of Morocco was en route to Washington, and Kennedy knew I'd met him a couple of times when I was covering North Africa and Hassan was only a prince. He wanted to know everything I knew about him and Morocco, which, not to put too fine a point on it, was a bit dated. He said he'd received a "damn good, well written" memo from CBS Washington bureau chief David Schoenbrun about Hassan. Kennedy said he was fascinated to read all the usual phrases

like "amusing, but not fun," "brave, but not courageous," reversed in Schoenbrun's memo, which described the Moroccan king as "courageous, but not
brave," and "funny, but not amusing." This led to a
discussion of writing and memoranda. Kennedy said
the best memo he had ever received—bar none—came
to him this week from Arthur Schlesinger on his four-
day trip to Europe, especially on the shadow of Prime
Minister Harold Wilson and Minister of Defense Den-
nis Healy. He promised to send it to me (but never
did).

Later, Kennedy took us into his office again to see
a new model ship, the *Flore,* presented to him by some
French naval officers, but basically by André Malraux.
He marveled at the workmanship and the speed with
which it had been made, though it looked to us like
just another model ship. When we went back upstairs,
Jackie put some Noel Coward-Gertrude Lawrence
music on the record player, and announced that
"Bunny" did a marvelous imitation of Coward. We
tried all night to get him to perform, but he wouldn't
do it.

Apropos of nothing we started talking about book
writing and Emmet Hughes. "It's a terrific book *(The
Ordeal of Power),*" the president announced. He
guessed that J. Edward Day, the postmaster general,
might have what he called "a Hughes-type book" in him,
but no one else in the administration. There had been
reports that Day was quitting, and I asked Kennedy
about his plans. He said he had no intention of replac-
ing him, but wondered "why, in heaven's name, the
postmaster general should be in the cabinet at all."

It was only 9:30 when Kennedy began to wind the
evening down, purposefully. "All right, Bear," he said

"John-John and JFK quite simply break each other up. Kennedy likes to laugh and likes to make people laugh, and his son is the perfect foil for him."

a couple of times to Tony, using our nicknames for each other, "let's put it on the road."

The Kennedy children had been carrying on during the cocktail hour. John-John—now two and a half years old—has a big thing about coming up to you and whispering a lot of gibberish in your ear. If you throw your head back in mock surprise, John-John roars with laughter until he drools. Kennedy keeps urging me to pick John-John up and throw him in the air, because he loves it so, and because Kennedy himself can't do it because of his back. "He doesn't know it yet," the president said, "but he's going to carry me before I carry him." Caroline came into the room with her wretched little dog, a Welsh Terrier named Charlie. When Kennedy came in a few seconds later, his first words were "Get that damn dog out of here, Buttons," as he calls Caroline.

The Kennedys seem remarkably good with their children considering what would appear to be the almost insuperable barriers of formality imposed on that relationship by the presidency. They see less of their children, obviously, but that doesn't seem to have interfered with the normal joy and gaiety that attractive children express in themselves and produce in their parents.

The president reacts to both children as if he were still guilty about being away from home so much on the campaign trail. He calls Caroline any night she is away from the White House in Newport or Palm Beach. Right after the inauguration, when Jackie was resting in Florida, JFK put in his nightly call to Caroline, only to be told by nurse Maud Shaw that Caroline had not yet returned from a friend's birthday party. "She's

With Caroline. "*The president reacts to both children as if he were still guilty about being away from home so much on the campaign trail. . . . One night when Kennedy [was] still a senator . . . [he] was soaking in the tub in their, Georgetown house. Caroline sailed in, threw a copy of* Newsweek *with JFK on the cover into the tub, shouting 'Daddy' gleefully.*

"*Now in the White House, they both feel Caroline is unspoiled. One night just as we were arriving off the elevator for dinner, Caroline streaked completely unembarrassed through the main upstairs hall, naked as a jaybird, chased by the completely embarrassed Miss Shaw.*"

got to start staying home at night," Kennedy told Miss Shaw, like the father of a wayward teen-ager.

Ever since the Kennedys realized that Caroline could read, and was in fact reading newspaper and magazine accounts of the family, they have been almost ferociously protective of her. They first realized Caroline's talent and proclivity one night when Kennedy, still a senator but campaigning hard, was soaking in the tub in their Georgetown house. Caroline sailed in, threw a copy of *Newsweek* with JFK on the cover into the tub, shouting "Daddy," gleefully.

Now in the White House, they both feel Caroline is unspoiled (one night just as we were arriving off the elevator for dinner, Caroline streaked completely unembarrassed through the main upstairs hall, naked as a jaybird, chased by the completely embarrassed Miss Shaw), but they are appalled by the national hunger for news and pictures of her and John-John, and wonder if they can keep them unspoiled. A recent reference on the "Ev and Charlie Show" (a TV regular featuring the Senate and House minority leaders, Everett Dirksen of Illinois and Charles Halleck of Indiana) to Caroline's overexposure has increased the president's concern.

Kennedy is as proud as any other parent of his daughter. Once Jackie framed a particularly gaudy group of finger paintings, blobs of red, yellow, and blue, and presented it to the president as the latest effort of their painter friend, Bill Walton. Jackie said shyly that she had paid $600 for it. Kennedy was stunned, not so much by the price as by the far-out abstract turn Walton had apparently taken. When Jackie confessed the artist was Caroline, he said simply, "Pretty good color."

MARK SHAW PHOTO

"*Right after the inauguration, when Jackie was resting in Florida, JFK put in his nightly call to Caroline, only to be told by nurse Maud Shaw that Caroline had not yet returned from a friend's birthday party. 'She's got to start staying home at night,' Kennedy told Miss Shaw, like the father of a wayward teenager.*

"*. . . Once Jackie framed a particularly gaudy group of finger paintings, blobs of red, yellow, and blue, and presented it to the president as the latest effort of their painter friend, Bill Walton. Jackie said shyly that she had paid $600 for it. Kennedy was stunned, not so much by the price as by the far-out abstract turn Walton apparently had taken. When Jackie confessed that the artist was Caroline, he said simply, 'Pretty good color.'*"

John-John and JFK quite simply break each other up. Kennedy likes to laugh and likes to make people laugh, and his son is the perfect foil for him.

"Everyone ought to run for office"

APRIL 2, 1963 / The dinner invitations we get to the White House come from Evelyn Lincoln, and they come late—almost always the same day, in the morning if we're lucky, but often as late as 5:00 or 6:00 P.M. Since we don't go out much at night it isn't much of a problem. The invitation for tonight came just after 6:00 P.M., and we ate with the Kennedys alone.

I'd spent a good part of the day working on a story about the use of lie detectors by the Pentagon. The president hadn't heard about it, and wanted all the details. Civilian and military officials in the Defense Department were being asked to take lie detector tests in the course of an investigation into who leaked—to Dick Fryklund, the *Washington Star*'s Pentagon correspondent—an Air Force report on how unnecessarily rough the investigators on the McClellan committee had been. Kennedy immediately called Salinger and asked him to call Zuckert and get Zuckert to knock the investigation off. Zuckert called the president a few seconds later, and Kennedy was very curt to him on the phone. "Let's stop doing it to ourselves, Mr. Secretary," he said. "This is hardly a question of national security, is it? Whoever leaked the report was trying to do us a favor, as far as I can see." When he hung up, Kennedy said Zuckert had claimed it was routine in an investigation of this kind to ask someone at the end of the questioning if he would be willing to take a lie detector test. "Boy, this is a big government," the president said, getting up out of his rocker with his arms flailing as he imitated a man trying to plug too many holes in one dike. "You push a button marked 'investigate,' and the whole giant machinery starts moving, and then you can't stop it." Salinger then called back and they talked briefly about the Pentagon spokesman, the kind and gentle Arthur Sylvester. "Arthur's days are numbered," Kennedy said. "I'll tell you that. He's a marvelous guy, but the trouble is he doesn't have the relationship with McNamara that I have with Salinger, where he can come busting into my office whenever he has to."

This led Kennedy to a discussion of his secretary of defense, and specifically of the recent release of some McNamara testimony in which he'd said that Bomarc missiles—which Canada has bought from the U.S.—serve no militarily useful purpose; they serve mostly to attract a few Soviet missiles. "Everyone ought to run for office," the president said, for the umpteenth time. "That's all there is to it." He revealed that McNamara's testimony had been subjected to four military reviews "and not a single military secret got through, but then this did." He said he had written McNamara a letter that morning, pointing out that he should quit while he's ahead, that he should "just lay off for a while," that he shouldn't worry, that there was no need to convince the committee that he was honest, and that the White House had received no mail on this subject.

Kennedy said he had been blistering many hides this week. He revealed he had called Linc White (State Department spokesman Lincoln White) at midnight to ask "Why the hell do we have to say that we tipped the British to the presence of anti-Castro raiders in the Bahamas?" In fact, the U.S. had asked England to support a joint surveillance against Cuban exile attacks on Cuba, and at our request the British had sent the frigate *Londonderry* on Cuban patrol for that purpose. Kennedy's point was that a man who had run for political office, as Linc White had not, would instinctively understand the political problems the British government would face if it became publicly known that Her Majesty had sent a frigate on patrol at the request of the U.S. government. Kennedy said he was still sizzling when he hung up on White, and so he called Bob Manning (former *Time* correspondent, then White's boss in the State Department, now editor of the *Atlantic Monthly*). Kennedy quoted Manning as saying he'd been out of town but would investigate, and when Manning called the president back it was only to say that he, too, felt that White had goofed. Kennedy thinks highly of Manning.

Our recent conversations about managed news had led to a *Newsweek* cover on the subject, and Kennedy told me he thought it was the best thing he had read on the subject—with two exceptions. First, he felt, we had not "tucked it to Arty" enough—another reference to his former friend, Arthur Krock of the *New York Times*, whom we had called "old and out of it." And second, he felt we should have used the word "fib" instead of "lie" in describing the administration's cover-up during the Cuban missile crisis. I told him he was really quibbling now, and he admitted he had not seriously objected to "lie."

Tony asked Kennedy how many people he saw in an average day, after we had been talking about human energy and vitality in ourselves and in our children.

I interrupted his list at one point to note that he had not mentioned any reporters, and he said that he really didn't see many reporters anymore. He had seen Mark Childs, he said (Marquis Childs, the distinguished *St. Louis Post-Dispatch* correspondent and columnist), and one foreign correspondent, whom he would not name. He said he had not seen Walter Lippmann since that dinner at our house right after the inauguration; he had not seen Reston, in spite of Reston's written request for an interview right after the steel strike settlement. He said he had answered Reston's request for an interview by suggesting that Reston interview Krock, who was posing as an informed observer of the Kennedy administration.

Kennedy said he had recently seen Harold Wilson and I told him I had, too, and found him to be a pretty cold fish. Kennedy said he agreed as a personal matter, but felt that everything Wilson said, including a recent speech to the National Press Club, "sounds just right." I told him about a lunch the British staged the previous Saturday with six U.S. reporters and Wilson at the home of Michael Robb of the British embassy. I asked him to guess which six American reporters the British had invited. After a few careful moments he came up with "Reston, Friendly, Hightower (John Hightower, the AP's diplomatic correspondent), Steele (John Steele, Time-Life bureau chief), Bradlee—and maybe Donovan." The actual list, I told him, was Phil Geyelin (diplomatic correspondent of the *Wall Street Journal*, now the Pulitzer Prize-winning editor of the *Washington Post*'s editorial page), Teddy White, David Brinkley of NBC, Schoenbrun, Reston, and me. Kennedy was sore that he had been that far off the mark.

Somewhere during the evening we got on the subject of pregnancy, and I asked Jackie if it were true that she was pregnant. She said she was not, but we think she is. We talked about how many more children Bobby and Ethel might have, and the president volunteered the advice that Tony and I should not have any more children, and advised, out of the blue, "You ought to get yourself cut."

From there we jumped somehow to the question of capital punishment. Kennedy told us about some man from Dubuque, Iowa,* who had called a doctor to his home late one night by pleading with him to visit his sick children and then murdered him in cold blood when he showed up. Appeal from his conviction had come all the way up to the president, and the governor of Iowa had been calling him. The president said he had asked Ed McDermott (Edward A. McDermott, director of the Office of Emergency Planning) to investigate, and McDermott had reported back that there was nothing the president could do. Apparently some provision of the Iowa constitution prevented the president from intervening, and the man had been executed. This reminded Kennedy of the first time he had been confronted with a mercy plea, a case soon after he took office involving a GI in Germany† who had raped an eleven-year-old girl twice and killed her. He had let this man be executed. I talked about my own interest in Judge David Bazelon (chief judge of the Court of Appeals for the District of Columbia) and his Durham Rule, which holds that a man shall not be held responsible for criminal acts committed as a result of a mental illness. It turned out we were all against capital punishment except the president. I asked him about the Catholic precept against taking a life, including abortions, and he said that he saw no conflict.

* His name was Victor Harry Feguer.
† Pvt. John A. Bennett.

He said he was all for people solving their problems by abortion (and specifically told me I could not use that for publication in *Newsweek*), and he didn't seem to equate execution with the taking of a life in the doctrinal sense.

The president was enthusiastic about his visit with King Hassan of Morocco. "He and the Shah, both of them playboys at one time," he said, "are so serious now that they are kings. They must be overcompensating." Hassan had given the president a gold sword studded with fifty diamonds. He unsheathed a similar jeweled sword that the Shah had given him, I unsheathed the Hassan sword, and we struck a dueler's pose, brandishing thousands of dollars worth of jeweled cutlery as if they were golf clubs. Jackie reported that she had written Hassan a five-page longhand letter in French. She also reported that she had asked her secretary, Pamela Turnure, to get her a kinescope of the recent "Meet The Press" show because someone had told her that Hassan—and Bradlee—were good. I told her I guessed it probably had one of the lowest ratings Lawrence Spivak (the show's producer and master of ceremonies) ever racked up.

Kennedy asked Jackie to pick one country out of three—Italy, Morocco, or Ireland—to spend a vacation in, if she could choose only one. She said she knew the president wanted to go to Ireland more than anything in the world, but she would choose Morocco.

The president asked me if he had ever told me the story of Diefenbaker (the Canadian prime minister) and the stolen document. He said the incident was at the root of all U.S.-Canadian problems. I told him he had not recounted that story, but that he could remedy that lack right now. If Diefenbaker lost the election Monday, he said, he would give me the story exclusively (talk about managed news!) and it was a block-buster. If Diefenbaker won? "Well, then, we'll just have to live with him," he said, and apparently no story.

"Let's sing a little song for Dad"

APRIL 9, 1963 / Tonight was really quite unforgettable when Ambassador Joe turned up as a dinner guest at the White House with the Kennedys, Bobby and Teddy, Eunice Kennedy Shriver, Ann Gargan, and us.

The old man is bent all out of shape, his right side paralyzed from head to toe, unable to say anything but meaningless sounds and "no, no, no, no," over and over again. But the evening was movingly gay, because the old man's gallantry shows in his eyes and his crooked smile and the steel in his left hand. And because his children involve him in their every thought and action. They talk to him all the time. They ask him "Don't you think so, Dad?" or "Isn't that right, Dad?" And before he has a chance to embarrass himself or the guests by not being able to answer, they are off on the next subject. Bobby and Teddy sang a little two-part harp harmony for him, after Bobby had suggested to Teddy "Let's sing a little song for Dad." It was calculatedly bad and off-key, but the ambassador leaned slightly forward in his wheelchair, tilted his head back to see them better, and was obviously delighted with their performance. For an encore, Teddy did his imitation of "Honey Fitz," bearing down on the falsetooth lisp, and everyone applauded, especially old Joe. Only he applauds with his eyes.

The ceremony making Winston Churchill an honorary American citizen had taken place that afternoon in the Rose Garden, and Kennedy senior had apparently caught a glimpse of it. The president teased his father about how "all your old friends showed up, didn't they, Dad?" It was obvious that by "all your old friends," Kennedy meant people who were high on the ambassador's enemies list: "Bernard Baruch," the president started listing them off. "Dean Acheson, he's on both the offense and the defense, isn't he, Dad?" Caroline and John-John were roaring around the living room, obviously oblivious to grandpa's condition, and equally obviously delighting him. At one point John-John careened into the small table on which the ambassador's drink was sitting, and dumped it smack into his lap. Tony and I were the only ones embarrassed. The truly remarkable Ann Gargan takes care of everything and she had him mopped off in a minute.

Going into dinner was a struggle. Jackie supported her father-in-law on one side, with Ann Gargan slightly behind him so that she can kick his right leg forward between steps. He can't do it himself. When he eats, he drools out of the right side of his mouth, but Jackie was wiping it off quickly, and by the middle of dinner there really was no embarrassment left. Kennedy senior had brought along crabs from Florida for dinner, and the president asked Tony to crack his for him. Apparently his back was giving him that much trouble.

"I must say," Kennedy said as he ate his crabs, "there is one thing about Dad: When you go with him you go first-class." There is a gaggle of agreement, and the ambassador, jabbing the air with his left hand, much as his son jabs the air with his right hand to make a point, says "No, no, no, no," and everyone knows what he means. In the old days it would have been some teasing wisecracks. Tonight it's a "no" that means "yes."

Jackie went to great pains to introduce me as "Beebo" Bradlee's son, since my father and Joe Kennedy had known each other slightly years ago, and the old man and I had talked about my father once when we were staying with the Kennedys at Palm Beach. "You remember your old friend Beebo," Jackie said to him. "You said how much better looking he was than Ben." He did recognize Tony and me; it was that obvious. His handshake with us was left-handed, but as strong as a football player's. Jackie seemed particularly good with the old man. She rattled on and on, talking to him about many things, especially reminding him how he and Judge Morrissey had worked on JFK to marry her.

After dinner the ambassador sank back into his wheelchair and stayed in the circle of conversation, at the center of it, really, for about half an hour. Then Ann Gargan announced that "Grandpa is going to bed." It was the only time the ambassador's "no, no, no" meant what it said, we all felt. Everybody came up to shake his hand, or kiss his head, and off he went. It was all so touching and simple and moving. The Kennedys are at their best, it sometimes seems, when they are family, and forthright and demonstrative, and they were at their best tonight.

The suicide of Charlene Wrightsman Cassini came up, after Joe Kennedy's presence had left our minds. She was the daughter of Charles Wrightsman, a millionaire Palm Beach neighbor of the Kennedys, and the wife of Igor Cassini, the New York society columnist who had been indicted in February for failing to register as an agent of the Trujillo government in the Dominican Republic. Kennedy told us she had written him only a few days ago, saying that they had no money, that their kids were being persecuted at school, that they seemed to have no future, and generally wondering what they were going to do. The president was obviously upset, and wondered out loud about the virtue of prosecuting Cassini. The Kennedys agreed that "Gigi was a jerk," but the president questioned the usefulness of putting him in jail now, and leaving all those children without a parent. Mrs. Cassini had apparently brought up a child by Cassini's first marriage, a child by her own first marriage, a child of Oleg Cassini, the dress designer and Igor's brother, and a child of their own. Her father, with all his money, Kennedy said, had refused to give her a cent since she married Cassini. Jackie revealed to us all that Igor "was on a walkout," apparently a jet set phrase to describe involvement with someone else.

The vote in Congress tomorrow to restore funds cut from the public works bills produced some Kennedy family disagreement. Teddy reported he had heard they had the votes to restore. Bobby reported to the contrary. And the president seemed to go along with his younger brother. Teddy kept pulling out a newspaper clipping from his briefcase, a piece by Bud Rogers of the *Boston Globe* giving Teddy significant credit for work behind the scenes in helping a mass transit bill to victory. Teddy was proud of the clipping, but the other Kennedys were giving him the bird about how lovingly he was already collecting clippings about himself. Teddy asked the family for their advice on the subject of his maiden speech in the Senate—unemploy-

ment, Massachusetts, or no speech at all. He got a lot
of noise, but no advice.

Someone asked about Pushinka, the puppy Khrushchev gave Caroline in June, 1961, a child of Strelka,
the dog the Soviets shot into orbit the year before, and
whether she was pregnant. The attorney general replied "No; we've been able to do everything else around
here, but we just haven't been able to get Pushinka
pregnant."

Diefenbaker's defeat—by Lester Pearson—was thor-
oughly explored. The trouble is that the president thinks
I know more about the allegedly stolen documents
and the blackmail, or whatever else is supposed to
have happened, than I do. I finally told him that, and
he arranged to have me drop by tomorrow, to live up
to his promise to give the inside skinny.

"Eyes Only, Secret, and Everything"

APRIL 10, 1963 / "Here it is," the president said, shov-
ing a fat file at me across his desk this afternoon, "Eyes
Only, Secret and Everything." I was there to get the
story behind Canadian Prime Minister Diefenbaker's
charges that the president of the United States had
written "S.O.B." on some official State Department
document concerning Diefenbaker and Canada.

The key document, classified Secret, is a memorandum from Walt Rostow to the president outlining
what the State Department hoped to accomplish during
Kennedy's visit to Canada in May, 1961. U.S. policy

Rostow argued, should be to "push" the Canadians: 1) to increase their Alliance for Progress contribution; 2) to join the Organization of American States; 3) to increase their foreign aid contribution and involvement, especially with the Indian consortium; and 4) to do more with the Neutrality Commission policing the uneasy truce in Laos.

One year later, in May, 1962, in a long, extraordinary letter to George Ball, who was then acting secretary of state, the U.S. ambassador to Canada, Livingston Merchant, described a ranting conversation he had had with Diefenbaker in which the Canadian p.m. revealed that he now possessed the original Rostow document (Kennedy guesses that someone on the U.S. delegation must have left it at a session with the Canadians, probably Bundy), that the letters "S.O.B." in the president's handwriting were on the document; that he and all Canadians would resent that, plus the word "push" if the document were made public; and that he intended to make it public as part of his political campaign for reelection. He told Merchant he had to release the document because Pearson and the Liberals were campaigning as the favorite party of the Kennedy administration, and Pearson himself had been to the White House for the Nobel Prize winners' dinner, and had seen Kennedy privately for half an hour beforehand. Diefenbaker was practically out of his mind with rage, Merchant reported.

The State Department's instructions back to Merchant four days later, closely following a special memorandum by Bundy and Ball, ordered the U.S. ambassador to go back to Diefenbaker and tell him that he would relay no such message to his government, especially to Kennedy, out of respect for Canada and Diefenbaker. Merchant was told to describe in detail what the U.S. reaction would be to this black-mail, and to tell Diefenbaker that Kennedy would not see him under any conditions, as Merchant had suggested.

Merchant reported back that it was his opinion that Diefenbaker, though still furious, would not release the document. And there the story lies. The president told me he did not write "S.O.B." on the Rostow document, and as evidence cited the fact that when Diefenbaker brought the whole thing up a year ago to Merchant, nothing was said about any "S.O.B." "At that time," Kennedy added, "I didn't think Diefenbaker was a son of a bitch. (Pause, for effect.) I thought he was a prick."

Kennedy wondered why the Canadian prime minister "didn't do what any normal, friendly government would do . . . make a photostatic copy, and return the original."

Act II of the steel crisis was also on Kennedy's mind, especially the coincidence of the dates, exactly one year after Act I, when U.S. Steel raised its prices, followed the next day by five other major steel manufacturers raising theirs. The president feels that his office and authority are being flouted, but he seems unsure what he should do about it, or can do about it. Basically, he feels the steel people are impossible. He calls them "those fuckers." A labor-management committee to work out a formula whereby some portion of a price increase would go to labor as its share, Kennedy said, might be possible if you were dealing with normal people, but not with steel people. The *Newsweek* expert on prices had doubted that the market would support a price rise at this time, but Kennedy dismissed that argument. "If foreign steel is imported," he said, "that would mean a loss of jobs here, and steel would then be hitting me over the head with other weapons." Kennedy revealed there was a special White House meeting at 6:00 that night, and called a man named "John" to ask him to be present.

On Laos, he again said there wasn't much the U.S. could do. He said we were moving up some supplies to Kong Le, but noted the irony of now putting all the American eggs in the basket of Souvanna Phouma, the man the Eisenhower administration had tried to discredit as a Communist.

The president was most interested in *Newsweek*'s story by Paris bureau chief Larry Collins about General Pierre Gallois' defection, and wanted to know where we had gotten the story. It apparently paralleled a secret cable from Paris, and Kennedy suspected that someone at the State Department had leaked it to us, despite the Paris dateline. I told him I knew it came from Paris, because I had been asked to check the story from here.

"You wouldn't shit me, would you?" he asked with a smile.

"Something about twenty-one or twenty-two"

APRIL 12, 1963 / I talked to the president briefly, in answer to a request to check back with him on the kind of story we were doing about Diefenbaker. He was in Palm Beach.

173

Diefenbaker still had not announced when he would leave office, but the president gave me a green light on the story, roughly along the lines of our discussion. He asked me to leave out something that I had failed to include—an insistence by Diefenbaker that Kennedy wait over to see him in Nassau.

I asked Kennedy quickly whether he knew anything about a possible resignation of Supreme Court Justice William O. Douglas, whose wife announced yesterday that she was filing for divorce. The president said he had heard reports that Douglas was going to resign from the Court, but that Douglas had told no one in the administration that he would, and Kennedy gave those reports no credence.

Kennedy said he heard Douglas "had something about twenty-one or twenty-two years old . . . think of that."

"You are my ideal, Jacqueline"

APRIL 29, 1963 / We dined alone with the Kennedys tonight, the first time since the news that Jackie was pregnant. It was plain that she had been pregnant two weeks ago when she told us she wasn't, but we felt it best not to bring that up. Tony was upset that she hadn't been told before the public announcement, until Jackie said that she hadn't even told her mother. She was plainly proud of having kept her secret. She's going to keep her figure, too. She hardly looks pregnant at all.

Jackie and Tony Bradlee in Newport. "Somewhere during the conversation, Jackie said to the president, 'Oh, Jack, you know you always say that Tony is your ideal.' The president replied, 'Yes, that's true,' and then a second or two later added, 'You're my ideal, Jacqueline'."

We were being used to referee another period of tension over family finances, the first we had heard since the night Kennedy blew his stack over "Department Stores . . . $40,000." It was less than $40,000 this time, the president said, but it was still high as hell. "Who's Mrs. Richard Cooper . . . art, $1400?" he asked Jackie, who was unable to identify Mrs. Cooper and squirmed uncomfortably as a result. She also said she had bought nothing except a couple of bathing suits. No dresses. She described what she had on as "this old thing which I bought two years ago for $60."

"Wouldn't you think it would cost us about what it cost us in Georgetown?" Kennedy asked, "considering all the things we get free here that we had to pay for there?" He said it costs "a fantastic amount more," despite the intervention of Carmine Bellino. "You feel better, just because it's less than $40,000," JFK said, a bit testily. He's really upset, but keeps a faintly amused and quizzical expression on his face as he beefs. We got into a discussion of how many people work for them at the White House and what they do, and that led us to George Thomas, the valet/butler. What does he really do, Tony asked, since he doesn't serve meals, only drinks. "He leads in the guy who brings breakfast," the president said, sourly.

The Kennedy children were much in evidence, Caroline in an angel costume and John-John careening around, as usual, bumping over his ginger ale twice and spilling everything he could get his hands on.

The subject of bills brought up the new country house being built in Atoka, Virginia, versus Camp David in the Catoctin mountains of Maryland. It's now obvious that the president likes Camp David, and has not much use for the new house. Jackie likes Camp

David now, and this is new, but she likes the new house for the expectation that it will give her an opportunity to do some hunting. Kennedy first objected to Camp David because he felt the presence of Marines patrolling the perimeters with dogs would be bad for the children. Now he said he likes the privacy, the separate houses where guests can be alone and out of his hair, and the heated swimming pool. He said we'd be asked up for a Camp David weekend soon.

We talked a great deal on the subject of men versus women, with special emphasis this time on women who castrate their husbands for various reasons. Somewhere during the conversation, Jackie said to the president "Oh, Jack, you know you always say that Tony is your ideal." The president replied "Yes, that's true," and then a second or two later added "You're my ideal, Jacqueline."

The Grand Duchess of Luxembourg was due in town shortly after dinner, and the president reported that Chicago's Mayor Richard Daley and his wife were going to spend the night at the White House during her visit. I said I had noticed that Peter Crotty (the Democratic leader from Buffalo, N.Y.) and Bob Wagner (the mayor of New York City) were both on the guest list with the Daleys for the state dinner in honor of the Grand Duchess, and asked the president how come. The purpose of a mixture of old line U.S. pols with a European duchess, and a grand duchess at that, didn't seem immediately obvious. "I have a feeling I'm going to be asking them for help pretty soon, and when I do, I don't want them saying 'Where have you been; we never saw you for the first three years of your term.'" Indications, like this one, are multiplying that Kennedy is looking forward to another run, and to the mandate he didn't get last time.

In this connection we discussed convention sites. Miami is definitely out, the president said: "Too many Cubans." Chicago doesn't want to pay for it, Kennedy answered when I said that Chicago looked like a shoo-in. "How about San Francisco?" he asked us, and we all agreed that would be great, considering that the next Democratic convention figured to be a dull one, and recreation would consequently be more important than usual.

As we left, the president showed us a lovely old engraving of Mount Vernon that he said was a birthday present to him from Bob and Margie McNamara. "Your present hasn't arrived yet, apparently," he said with a grin.

The McNamaras had heard that the Kennedys had seen this engraving and admired it. It must have cost a bundle.

"I can't believe we'll be that lucky"

MAY 9, 1963 / Bobby Kennedy was on the telephone trying to raise $160,000 bail for people imprisoned in Montgomery, Alabama, during Dr. Martin Luther King's desegregation march, when we arrived for dinner at the White House tonight. The other guests: Joe Kennedy, Sr., Ann Gargan, and Teddy Kennedy. The attorney general said the Alabama authorities had refused to take a bond and were insisting on cash bail, and insisting that the cash be raised in Alabama. He told us he had called George Meany, head of the AFL-CIO, and Dave McDonald, head of the steel workers, and while we were talking he took a call from Labor Secretary Arthur Goldberg.

Old Joe was unchanged. It took us a few minutes to get used to his "no, no, no," again, but we did.

The president came in late (he had generally just finished a swim at this time of the evening) and quickly asked Bobby if he had given me my "scoop" . . . which turned out to be that Jimmy Hoffa and the Teamsters had invested "hundreds of thousands of dollars" in William Loeb's Manchester, N.H., *Union-Leader*. "You ought to get the Pulitzer Prize for that one," he said, in one of the few totally naive statements I ever heard him make about our business. Not only are magazines ineligible for Pulitzer Prizes, which I would have bet my bottom dollar Kennedy knew, but "the scoop" was something a little less than advertised. Hoffa's "investment" was in fact a loan to Loeb, and its existence had been published in a New England publisher's journal and was about to be published in *Editor & Publisher,* the newspaper weekly.

Early in the evening, the president asked his usual question about next week's *Newsweek* cover story, and when he heard it was Barry Goldwater he said "I can't believe we will be that lucky," and then he added "I can't believe Barry will be that lucky either. The trouble is that if he's the nominee, people will start asking him questions, and he's so damn quick on the trigger that he will answer them. And when he does, it will be all over."

We got on the subject of family backgrounds, and the president noted with pride that he and his brothers and sisters were 100 percent pure Irish. Their grandfathers were Kennedy, Fitzgerald, Hickey, and Hannon. He noted with glee how "mongrelized you all are," pointing to Tony (English and French), me (English, German, and Polish), and Jackie (English and French). He changed the subject when we pointed out that if Jackie were all that "mongrelized," so were Caroline and John.

Kennedy asked us about our summer plans, which were very much up in the air, since we were exploring how we could make the trip with him to Ireland. I said that we were having troubling getting Tony accredited to write for some newspaper (she had written a couple of pieces for the *Boston Globe* when the Kennedys visited France and Vienna to see Khrushchev) so that we could finance her trip again. The president immediately asked her to go with him on his plane, and I just as immediately nixed that as an impropriety. "Jesus, you said that fast," Kennedy said, apparently impressed more by the speed than the morality.

"Congress? They're impossible"

MAY 21, 1963 / We were shunted swiftly by a fleet of butlers into the family living room when we arrived for dinner tonight with the Kennedys alone. The occasion was a cocktail party given by the Kennedys in the Oval Room for some of the astronauts and their wives. Before the Kennedys joined us, Steve and Jean Smith showed up and we figured they were going to have dinner, too. But Steve refused to bust into the astronaut party, and Jean said she didn't dare do it by herself.

As a result, strangely we thought, they had one drink with us and left.

When the Kennedys did arrive, Tony and I were sitting side by side on the sofa. Jack entered, saying "How sweet," and called back the photographer who had been taking pictures of the astronauts. The result was a color photograph of the four of us on the sofa. (Jackie gave it to us a week or so later, after carefully inking in a little more skirt, because she felt the picture showed too much of her legs.)

Kennedy identifies enthusiastically with the astronauts, the glamour surrounding them and the courage and skill it takes to do their jobs. He knows them quite well by now, and recognizes them individually with ease. He said two or three times that evening that he finds Rene Carpenter the most attractive of the wives. He called Shepard and Glenn "the personality boys," and he said he'd just been lobbied by the astronauts for another Mercury shot, presumably with Shepard aboard. He said he'd suggested that Slayton accompany the first Gemini shot. Jackie told us she had broken the ice at the cocktail party by saying when she came into the room "You're all doing what I did for the first two years in this place . . . you're whispering," and then she apparently broke up the group by asking them if they knew Sigismund von Braun, Werner von Braun's brother who had figured recently and juicily in the divorce case of the Duke of Argyll. Jackie was impressed with the way the astronauts' wives banded together so often out of necessity.

The Kennedy kids arrived on schedule and the president was quickly down on his hands and knees with John-John. He becomes more and more involved with that child, shouting "I'm going to get you" and tickling him until he wets his pants with uncontrolled delight.

181

"When the Kennedys did arrive, Tony and I were sitting side by side on the sofa. Jack entered, saying, 'How sweet,' and called back the photographer who had been taking pictures of the astronauts. The result was a color photograph of the four of us on the sofa. (Jackie gave it to us a week or so later, after carefully inking in a little more skirt, because she felt the picture showed too much of her legs.)"

It's wonderful to watch him take such new delight in one of the older pleasures known to man.

Much of the evening was devoted to the upcoming trip to Europe, and especially his visit to Ireland. This is the part that he really looks forward to. The rest of the trip is political. Ireland is pure heart. He was indignant when I told him we wished the trip were in reverse, beginning in Ireland and ending up in Rome, since we were trying to fix it so that we could stay in Europe after he left and would rather end up in Positano on the Amalfi Drive than in New Ross in the middle of the Irish nowhere. "Goddamn it," the president said. "You've got some Irish in you. Dave Powers tells me so, and you've both got to go to Ireland." Kennedy renewed his offer to take Tony along on his own plane, and the offer was again refused. Jackie spoke most romantically about Ireland, and reminisced about a trip she had taken there with her stepbrother ("Yusha" Auchincloss). Kennedy repeated, with delight, the story in the papers about the mayor of New Ross, where Kennedy's ancestors had lived, telling all the residents not to clean up for the president's visit, not to take the manure from the front steps to the back, saying "If he wants chrome, he can find it on Madison Avenue." Tony told him that we had been thinking of doing a story based on interviews with the citizens of New Ross after he left about what they really thought of the local boy who had made so good. He saw little merit in the idea.

We talked about the wheat referendum, and Agriculture Secretary Orville Freeman called him shortly after 10:00 P.M. to tell him that they were licked. "You can't get 66 2/3 percent of the American people to agree on anything," Kennedy said with great frustration. "And as for Congress, they're impossible. Ever since Roosevelt's day all the laws have been pretty much written down, and all the Senate investigations and hearings don't amount to much." He singled out McClellan as a particularly "overtly useless" senator. And he complained about how often, and over what minor issues, he had to cash checks with the Congress. Today, he cited as an example, he'd had to call Ev Dirksen, the Senate minority leader, on the subject of coffee parity. The president said he felt that a better system would have Congress approve plans from the Executive Department, and then throw them out after four years if they didn't like them.

We watched NBC's special on the Kremlin in Jackie's bedroom while the president walked around in his underdrawers and wondered what life must be like in that mausoleum. Jackie told us about the day that Bobby Kennedy had called the Kremlin in a rage about something, a story that had been kicking around town for some time and had been denied often. He was apparently calling Georgi N. Bolshakov, the Washington press corps' and the New Frontier's favorite Soviet diplomat, who was carried on the Soviet embassy's rolls as a journalist but who was felt by all of us to be a spy, like all Soviet diplomats. If so, he was a gregarious spy, could drink up a storm, and liked to arm wrestle. Anyway, Jackie was now confirming the story that had been so often denied. But, she reported, there had been no answer at the Kremlin when the United States attorney general had called late at night.

We then watched the 11:00 P.M. news together. JFK was appalled at the eagerness displayed by Clinton Anderson, the Democratic senator from New Mexico, who was head of the Senate space committee, and by Vice-President Johnson to be photographed for TV with astronaut Gordon Cooper after the White

"Kennedy sometimes referred to Lyndon Johnson, and truly without hostility, as a 'riverboat gambler,' and often as 'Landslide,' a reference to the time when LBJ was first elected to the Senate by a majority in the primary of eighty-seven votes.

". . . Kennedy is funny about LBJ. He really likes his roguish qualities, respects him enormously as a political operator, a politician who can get things done, and he thinks Lady Bird is 'neat.' But there are times—like to-night—when LBJ's simple presence seems to bug him. It's not very noble to watch, and yet there it is."

House ceremony earlier today. (Cooper had just completed twenty-two orbits of the earth.) Kennedy told us that "Landslide" (Lyndon Johnson) was going up to New York with the astronauts tomorrow—on his own. The president had not asked him to go. This seemed a little petty of Kennedy. Kennedy had given Johnson special responsibilities in connection with the space program, and his presence in New York with the astronauts seemed perfectly logical. Kennedy is funny about LBJ. He really likes his rougish qualities, respects him enormously as a political operator, a politician who can get things done, and he thinks Lady Bird is "neat." But there are times—like tonight —when LBJ's simple presence seems to bug him. It's not very noble to watch, and yet there it is. When a bright-eyed young child showed up on the television screen, Kennedy shouted "My God, that's Bobby Shriver," his nephew and the son of Eunice and Sargent Shriver. "He's the biggest publicity hound we've got around here." He grabbed for the telephone and asked the operator to get him one of the adult Shrivers "if they're not asleep." In a couple of seconds he had Sarge Shriver on and, with a distinct edge in his voice, gave him the business about young Bobby hogging the camera.

Governor George Wallace was next on the news with his "bar the door" speech,* and the president grew quickly solemn. "He's just challenging us to use the marshals," he said gloomily. "That's going to be something."

---

* On May 21, 1963, U.S. District Court Judge Hobart H. Grooms ruled that the University of Alabama had to admit two black students who had applied. That same night, Wallace said in a news conference in Montgomery: "I will be present to bar the entrance of any Negro who attempts to enroll at the University of Alabama."

There was discussion of the president's upcoming birthday party on the twenty-ninth. It's going to be held on the yacht *Sequoia,* not the *Honey Fitz* as the president wanted, because the *Honey Fitz* is in trouble. "She's got rotting stern timbers," the president announced, and then added "like the rest of us, I guess." Jackie's worried because *Sequoia* "seats only twenty-six for dinner."

Charlie Bartlett called during the evening to tell the president about some memorandum he'd just seen which showed that George Romney was not only running for president, but could win. (A story apparently based on this memo showed up in the papers a few days later.) Kennedy reacted indignantly to the idea of Romney as president. "What federal services would he cancel?" the president asked incredulously. "What new civil rights legislation does he think he could pass that we can't pass?"

"Not three French wines. Only one—domestic"

MAY 22, 1963 / Jackie called me at the office this afternoon to complain about a single sentence in the current issue of *Newsweek,* which said that three French wines had been served at the president's lunch for Alabama editors last week.

Not true, she said. "It was not three French wines. It was only one, and it was domestic." Apparently the White House has been taking some flack about too many French wines being served, and too much French being used to describe the menus. And so she had ordered the staff not to call any dish by its French name anymore. At issue was "Oeufs Mollet à la reine," henceforth to be known simply as "Eggs Mollet."

On the question of the wine, she was definitely right and *Newsweek* was wrong, we learned after investigating. Chuck Roberts, our distinguished White House correspondent, translated "Almaden Cabernet Sauvignon" as three French wines, the only mistake I ever knew him to make.

"Come in Yachting Clothes"

MAY 29, 1963 / The invitations to the president's birthday party, a cruise down the Potomac on the *Sequoia,* had read "Come in Yachting Clothes," which meant white pants as far as I was concerned. In addition to the Kennedys, the guests included Bobby and Ethel, Teddy, a *Last Hurrah* type from Boston named Clem Norton, who had been a friend and coatholder of Honey Fitz, the Shrivers, Bill Walton, Mary Meyer, a woman introduced only as Enid, Lem Billings, George Smathers and his wife, Red and Anita Fay, Charlie and Martha Bartlett, the actor David Niven and his wife Hjordis, Jim Reed, Fifi Fell and ourselves. A three-piece band played all night.

After cocktails on the fantail, with thunder and lightning as omens for the rains to come, dinner was served below. There was a bunch of toasts, including

Red Fay's vaudeville act in which he sings, if that's the word, "Hooray for Hollywood." This act panics the Kennedys, and they've heard it a hundred times. No one else quite understands why. Throughout the toasts, the Kennedys—except for Jackie—heckle whoever is on his feet with boos, catcalls, cheers—mostly boos. The boor of the evening turned out to be Clem Norton, whom Teddy had brought along at the last minute and who does endless imitations of Honey Fitz that mean very little to anyone who is neither a Fitzgerald nor a Kennedy. Norton got more stewed by the hour, until at midnight he was literally stumbling over the presents piled in front of the president. There was a moment of stunned silence as Norton lurched forward and put his shoe right through a beautiful, rare old engraving that was Jackie's birthday present to her husband. It had cost more than $1,000 and Jackie scoured galleries to find it, but she greeted its destruction with that veiled expression she assumes, and when everyone commiserated with her over this disaster, she just said "Oh, that's all right. I can get it fixed."

Kennedy has not gotten the word that the "twist" is passé; any time the band played any other music for more than a few minutes, he passed the word along for more Chubby Checkers. He was also passing the word all night to the *Sequoia*'s captain. Apparently through an abundance of caution in case he wasn't having a good time, Kennedy had ordered the skipper of the *Sequoia* to bring her back to the dock at 10:30 P.M., only to be ordered back out "to sea"—which meant four or five miles down the Potomac. This happened no less than four times. The weather was dreadful most of the evening, as one thunderstorm chased us up and down the river all night, and everyone was more or less drenched. Teddy was the wettest, and on top of everything mysteriously lost one leg of his trousers some time during the night.

At one point during the toasts, George Smathers rose and delivered a particularly laudatory eulogy of the president that embarrassed most of the guests. First, because the tone of most of the toasts had been gently, and not so gently, teasing, and second, because the senator from Florida had spent a good bit of the previous year working against various New Frontier legislative proposals on the Hill.

It took Bobby to pipe up and say what everyone else was thinking. "Where were you when we needed you, George?" he asked. "You weren't with us in 1962, that's for sure." The president led the roar of laughter that followed.

"Do you think you could get used to this kind of life?"

MAY 30, 1963 / We gathered on the south lawn of the White House about noon, all of us a touch hung over from last night's gaieties, for a helicopter ride to Camp David, our first ride in the president's chopper and our first trip to Camp David. With us were the Nivens, Caroline and John-John and their nurse, Miss Shaw, Skipper the German Shepherd dog, Captain Tazewell Shepard, the president's naval aide, and a flock of Secret Service men.

It was the beginning of an extraordinary day for us. The Nivens were charming, and though they had known none of us before last night, it was like a gathering of old friends. On the way up in the helicopter, the president turned to me and said "Do you think you could get used to this kind of life? Pretty hard to take, isn't it?"

When we arrived, each of us went to small individual cabins. Ours was "Maple," with a living room, one very small bedroom, one large bedroom and two baths. We rallied ten minutes later in front of the main lodge, and Kennedy drove us all to a skeet shooting range near the heliport. The president shot first, and he was as lousy as we all turned out to be. He hit about four of the first twenty, but no one else did much better. Niven made us all laugh as he explained his theory that the entire secret of skeet shooting was in the voice one used to order up the clay pigeons. Whereupon he would whisper "High Tower, pull" . . . and miss, then shout "Low Tower, pull," and miss again.

We then went for a swim in the pool, heated, of course. The president gave his bathing trunks to Niven and went in in his skivvies. He wore his back brace, even for the short walk from the dressing room to the pool. His back had been giving him real trouble, he admitted, but was almost "miraculously better" last night and today. Jackie told us that she had asked Dr. Janet Travell, the back wizard, for some shot that would take Kennedy's back pain away, if only just for the birthday party. She had said there was such a shot, but it would remove all feeling below the waist. "We can't have that, can we, Jacqueline?" the president had ruled. The president said Dr. Travell had been great for him, until this particular pain, which she had been unable to cure.

During the swim, just Kennedy, Niven, and myself, the president ranged over a wide variety of subjects:

"We gathered on the south lawn of the White House about noon, all of us a touch hung over from last night's gaieties, for a helicopter ride to Camp David. With us were the Nivens, Caroline and John-John and their nurse, Miss Shaw, Skipper, the German Shepherd dog, Captain Tazewell Shepard, the president's naval aide, and a flock of Secret Service men. . . . On the way up in the helicopter, the president turned to me and said, 'Do you think you could get used to this kind of life? Pretty hard to take, isn't it?' "

"Kennedy drove us all to a skeet shooting range near the heliport. The president shot first, and he was as lousy as we all turned out to be. . . . Niven made us all laugh as he explained his theory that the entire secret of skeet shooting was in the voice one used to order up the clay pigeons. Whereupon he would whisper 'High Tower, pull' . . . and miss, then shout 'Low Tower, pull,' and miss again."

political giving, the Olympics, and yachting among them. He remarked that the only people who really gave during political campaigns now were Jews. This reminded him that Hugh Auchincloss, his wife's stepfather, had been approached for a political donation in 1960. His "gift," the president said with ill-disguised feeling, was a promise not to give any money to the Republicans this year, as he did normally. "Eventually the old boy came up with a magnificent 500 bucks," he added. Dick Dilworth (Richardson K. Dilworth, mayor of Philadelphia) had once asked his old friend, Harold Vanderbilt, for a contribution when he ran for governor of Pennsylvania, Kennedy told us, and he, too, had come away with a whopping $500.

The president said he looked forward to the day when the government would give each candidate ten million dollars and leave it at that. "I spent thirteen million dollars in 1960," he revealed, and ended up with a huge deficit. "If the government gave you ten million dollars, you could spend that and then go out and raise another ten or twenty." As high on the hog as we were currently sitting, the conversation had a heavy dose of the unreal.

Harold Vanderbilt's name led Kennedy to a discussion of yachting, particularly how impressed he had been by the fact that the Soviets had won the Star class races in the last Olympics, even though they had raced them for only a few years. And this reminded him of a story about how the New York Yacht Club had forced the resignation of some British lord who had falsely charged the Americans with illegally ballasting its candidate in the America's Cup races.

After the swim, with the Nivens not yet present, the four of us got on the subject of a guest at the birthday party last night (who shall here be nameless), who had told Jackie and Tony that he had not slept with his wife for the last sixteen years. This kind of dirt the president of the United States can listen to all day long.

We adjourned for Bloody Marys on the terrace, which overlooks a sloping lawn and a valley that extends forever southward. All the presents rescued from the rain and rumpus of the night before had been piled around the president's chair for him to open. The lovely old engraving, punctured by Clem Norton's clodhoppers and really ruined, was the only low point of the festivity. Kennedy seemed not to understand that it had been ruined the night before. He simply put it to one side, saying "That's too bad, isn't it, Jackie?" and moved on to the next present. Jackie was almost as unemotional about what would have been, we felt, a disaster to most people. They both so rarely show any emotion, except by laughter.

The president's presents varied all the way from beautiful, expensively bound books to the junkiest presents sent to the White House by strangers last week, and specially culled by Jackie for his pleasure. The hands-down junkiest was a giant pop art picture of the president printed on an ordinary bed sheet. The present he seemed to like the most was a scrapbook from Ethel, which was a parody of the White House tours with their own Hickory Hill madhouse substituted for the White House. Kennedy ripped the wrappings of his presents with the speed and attention of a four-year-old child, only to cast each aside and start unwrapping the next one.

After lunch, the president retired for his ritual nap and Niven and I played golf on the front lawn. There is one green, with four or five tees tucked into different parts of the surrounding woods. Then we joined his wife, Jackie, and Tony, who were working on yet another bottle of Soave. The Nivens had to leave at 4:00 P.M., and we drove them down to the heliport to see them off.

Back in the main lodge Kennedy was up, and we went for another swim. After the swim, cocktails; after cocktails, dinner; and then after dinner instead of spending the night as planned, the president announced he had to return, and we all flew back to Washington.

"If the Russians want to build Skybolt, good luck to them"

JULY 6, 1963 / I called the president this morning and reached him in Hyannisport, the first time we had talked since he had returned from his trip to Germany, Ireland, Britain, and Italy. He said he wished we had been in Ireland, but he talked only briefly about his trip. I had spent the Fourth of July holiday in the slums of the south side of Chicago polling with Lou Harris, and told Kennedy all about it, at his insistence, as usual.

I asked him if he could shed any light on reports we were hearing of a "megaton" scandal brewing in Great Britain, but got nowhere. I told him we had heard that plans for the Skybolt missile left by Bob McNamara in December with the British had found their way to the Soviets. The president's only comment was "If the Russians want to build Skybolt, good luck to them." Otherwise he had nothing to add or detract from the story.

I also asked him for a little "guidance" on a story by Walter Trohan of the *Chicago Tribune* and Mark Childs that he and Khrushchev had exchanged some forty secret letters. "That's a lot of crap," Kennedy replied quickly, but I'm not so sure Trohan and Childs aren't at least technically correct. The president said that since the first of the year (1963) there had been maybe four or five or six letters. There had been five or six involved in Cuba alone, the previous year. The existence of all the letters, he thought, was public knowledge, even though the contents might not be public. And he said there was nothing startling in any of them that still might be secret. But later the president said that if by forty letters people meant twenty separate exchanges, and if routine greetings and congratulations were included, it was possible that the figure forty was "pretty accurate."

"You could carry Bombay the way you carry Boston"

SEPTEMBER 12, 1963 / We went to Newport with the Kennedys for a long weekend today, flying up in Air Force One in his luxurious private compartment. Air Force sergeants stand ready to bring you anything you want to drink or eat, the latest copies of all magazines, and every edition of several papers. Claiborne Pell (the senator from Rhode Island) and the two Rhode Island congressmen rode up front with the Secret Service. The president arrived thirteen minutes late, timidly carrying a felt hat. I had never seen him wear a hat, but he told us "I've got to carry one for a while . . . they tell me I'm killing the industry."

On the way up Taz Shepard slipped him papers from a large black folder, and the president slipped me a few here and there. One was a letter from Chester Bowles, never a particular favorite of JFK's, who had been under secretary of state and was now the American ambassador to India. (Kennedy had once told me a story, with relish, about Bobby and Chet Bowles. It appears that Bobby had heard Bowles quoted as saying he wasn't sure he was with the administration in their handling of the early days of the Cuban missile crisis. When they next met, Bobby went over to Bowles, grabbed him by the coat collar and said "I want you to know something. You're with us in this all the way, right?" It had apparently been tense.) Bowles was reporting on a poll taken in New Delhi by an organization friendly to V. K. Krishna Menon, India's minister of defense, and therefore not particularly friendly to the United States. The poll showed that 43 percent of those polled felt that the U.S. was the country they most admired, with 13 percent for the United Kingdom and 11 percent for Japan and the Soviet Union. Another poll showed that 37 percent of those polled said Kennedy was the man they most admired, compared to only 33 percent for Nehru and 8 percent for Khrushchev. "You could carry Bombay the way you carry Boston," Bowles concluded. "You can use that one anytime, Benjy," Kennedy said generously.

Another letter was from Seymour Harris, a professor of political economics at Harvard, to Kermit Gordon, Kennedy's budget bureau director, suggesting that the government examine its expenditures on the basis of the number of jobs created per dollar spent. Some expenditures of billions create comparatively few jobs, Harris was saying, while other expenditures of only a few hundred million create many more jobs. (*Newsweek* made small stories out of both of these letters.)

We arrived at Quonset Naval Air Station, where Kennedy warned us as he got up to leave the plane that he had a "little toe dance to do" with Rhode Island's Republican governor, John Chafee, who was meeting the president at the airport. He suggested we go right to the helicopter waiting to take us to Newport, which we did, and when he joined us he was steaming at Chafee. First, because he had given the Kennedys a rather tacky, uninscribed, unadorned silver-plated bowl for an anniversary present, for this was the Kennedys' tenth wedding anniversary; and second, for making him go through the entire welcoming ceremony, speeches and all, twice. The TV cameraman had been accidentally shut out of the first ceremony. "Boy, he learns fast," the president said to us and to Pell. "I didn't have that much brass until I'd been in Congress five years . . . pushing a president around like that." All weekend the president steamed about the incident, and kept trying to think of diabolical ways to get even, or "put him in his place."

The helicopter took off in a dark overcast for the jump across the bay. Halfway across, the president spotted the crew of a carrier lined up at attention along the deck, presumably in his honor, and asked the chopper pilot to circle low over the carrier to show that he was aware and appreciative of their respect. The Navy has a special hold on him, irrespective of his rank as commander-in-chief. We landed on the lawn of Hammersmith Farm, in a scene that was half space-age pomp and half *Wuthering Heights*. The wind whistled from the helicopter blades, but the light was the dark yellow light of a New England fall evening, and that great barn of a house could have been brought over intact from a Brontë moor. This was the first time we had seen Jackie since the death of little Patrick, and she greeted JFK with by far the most affectionate embrace we had ever seen them give each other. They are not normally demonstrative people, period.

As we sorted ourselves out in the main hall, the president offered the tacky silver bowl he had just received from Governor Chafee to his mother-in-law, saying that he had long wanted to give her a token of his undying affection. Mrs. Auchincloss cooed like a Helen Hokinson dove, completely convinced that Kennedy was serious . . . even when she gazed in dismay at the bowl itself.

Presents—anniversary presents this time—were opened at cocktails before dinner with the Kennedys, the Auchinclosses, Jackie's stepbrother and sister, Yusha and Janet Auchincloss, Sylvia Blake, the Newport wife of Bob Blake, a foreign service officer then stationed in the Congo, and ourselves. We gave them a pair of antique tole trays—fifty bucks worth—which Jackie seemed to like but which left the president comfortably cool, we felt. The Auchinclosses gave them a fancy metal tree which held a lot of candles. Sylvia Blake gave them some place mats with ships on them, and Yusha gave them some books, but the *pièces de résistance* were their presents to each other.

Kennedy produced as his present to Jackie a letter from Klejman (J. J. Klejman, the New York antiquities dealer) listing all the unique antiques he had in stock, with a description (and price) for each, telling his wife that she could have any one she wanted. None cost less than $1,000, and though he didn't read out the prices as he read the descriptions, he would whisper to us "Got to steer her away from that one" as he came to those that were particularly expensive. There were some Dégas and Fragonard drawings, but mostly there were pre-Christian statues and Etruscan *objets d'art* from the second century B.C., an Egyptian head, two necklaces, a Thai bracelet. She finally chose a simple coiled serpent bracelet.

Jackie gave the president a scrapbook of before and

"[The Kennedys] are the most remote and independent people we know most of the time, and so when their emotions do surface it is especially moving."

after pictures of the Rose Garden at the White House. On each page there was a picture of what the garden had looked like that day, plus a thermofax copy of his schedule that day, plus a quotation in her own handwriting, often from Joe Alsop's landmark column on gardening,* and occasionally a press headline. The president read all the quotations aloud, pausing to admire Joe's ornate prose. He relished notable writing, and has ever since he started collecting examples of good prose and putting them in a bound book, which he was still doing when he started running for president.

Dinner was on the dicey side. Jackie's stepfather is not exactly a swinger, and the toasts were pretty much in his image. We were high on the hog again, with much wine, caviar, and champagne, but we all went to bed soon after dinner. Just before we retired Jackie drew me aside, her eyes glistening near tears, to announce that "you two really are our best friends." It was a forlorn remark, almost like a lost and lonely child desperately in need of any kind of friend. She repeated the message a couple of times to Tony during the weekend, citing particularly our letters to them about the baby's death. I had forgotten what I had written—it had been a bad summer for our friends, with Patrick's death and the sudden, jolting suicide of Phil Graham, whose light finally burned too bright and destroyed him—but Jackie said it was a description of an instant of love we had seen between a father and

---

* This column appeared in March, 1962, filled with awe and anticipation of Spring. "Watching the new green cover a box bush," Alsop wrote in a leap only he could make, "is just as exciting as watching the progress of the anti-guerrilla effort in South Vietnam. But in the reporter's trade, alas, the anti-guerrilla efforts have to be covered more intensively than the old earth's annual effort of self-renewal." No one but Joe Alsop could strike that metaphor, and make it stick.

a small baby, parting in Naples. They are the most remote and independent people we know most of the time, and so when their emotions do surface it is especially moving.

The next day we went out for a cruise late in the morning. Kennedy would occasionally check large ships that we passed to see if they had collected the crew at attention to pay him proper respect. The biggest yacht any of us had ever seen let us pass un-noticed, and the president insisted on knowing the name of the ship and the name of its owner, and with mock indignation the president vowed to "get him." Unfortunately, the captain of our ship was unable to identify the owner. (But the president got a report from his naval aide later that night. The ship belonged to Daniel K. Ludwig, the enormously rich shipbuilder.)

The president and I played golf one afternoon at the Newport Country Club, and this is always a harrowing experience for me. In the first place, if you play golf with a president you are apt to play at some fancy country club whose code of dress requires clothes that I do not have in my wardrobe . . . like golf shoes, for openers. As a result I hit off the first tee in old sneak-ers, and I feel like three down before I hit a shot. In the second place, if you play golf with a president you are dead sure to be watched by a crowd of people who either play golf better than you do and therefore you know they're going to laugh when you shank the ball, or line the roads and shout to be recognized by your partner. In any case, that's another two down. In the third place, there are Secret Service men all around you, carrying guns in dummy golf bags, and that doesn't do anything for your game. And finally, if you play golf with this president, his patience is so

"The president and I played golf one afternoon at the Newport Country Club, and this is always a harrowing experience for me. In the first place, if you play golf with a president you are apt to play at some fancy country club whose code of dress requires clothes that I do not have in my wardrobe . . . like golf shoes, for openers. As a result I hit off the first tee in old sneakers, and I feel like three down before I hit a shot."

limited that you can never stop to look for a lost ball, and that doesn't suit my game at all.*

But Kennedy is fun to play golf with, once you get out of sight of·the sightseers, primarily because he doesn't take the game seriously and keeps up a running conversation. If he shanks one into the drink, he could let go with a broad-A "bahstard," but he would be teeing up his next shot instantly. With his opponent comfortably home in two and facing a tough approach, he might say "No profile needed here, just courage," a self-deprecating reference to his book *Profiles in Courage*. When he was losing, he would play the old warrior at the end of a brilliant career, asking only that his faithful caddy point him in the right direction, and let instinct take over. He could play TV golf com-

---

* I remember particularly well two other golf games with the president. Once in Palm Beach I was playing with Joe Kennedy against the president and Earl T. Smith, a Palm Beach neighbor, millionaire, and onetime U.S. ambassador to Cuba. Despite the money which the other members of the foursome had, the stakes were set by the ambassador at ten cents a hole. On the eighteenth tee Mr. Kennedy and I were two up, meaning that if we won the last hole we'd win thirty cents each, and if we lost it we'd still win a dime each. Kennedy and Smith wanted "to make it interesting" and wanted to play the last hole for a dollar, which even I could afford. But the ambassador was having none of it. "Why should we?" he asked his son. "This way we're going to win at least ten cents. Your way we could lose eighty cents." Maybe that's why he's so rich.

Another time Kennedy and I were playing at Hyannisport with Ethel, and she was about seven months pregnant. I had not played golf for a couple of years, as I remember, and I had never played that course. The stakes were again ten cents a hole. Once I asked Ethel what club she thought I should use, because I was unfamiliar with the course and unsure of my own judgment. She suggested a five iron, and I clocked it pretty good, only to see it go sailing away over the green. I turned around to the sound of gales of laughter from Ethel and the president. She wanted to win so badly she had purposely suggested too much club.

The president and Chuck Spalding (left) *watch while
Pierre Salinger lofts one off the third tee at Hyannisport.
The ball obviously has gone nearly straight up—and there
is a peat marsh in its immediate future. "Kennedy is fun
to play golf with, once you get out of sight of the sightseers. . . . If he shanks one into the drink, he could let go
with a broad-A 'bahstard,' but he would be teeing up his
next shot instantly. With his opponent comfortably home
in two and facing a tough approach, he might say, 'No
profile needed here, just courage,' a self-deprecating reference to his book,* Profiles in Courage."

mentator as he hits the ball, saying, "With barely a glance at the packed gallery, he whips out a four iron and slaps it dead to the pin." He is competitive as hell, with a natural swing, but erratic through lack of steady play.

Jackie once gave the president a golf course for his birthday. It was at Glen Ora, the estate of Mrs. Raymond Tartière which they used as a weekend retreat during 1961 and 1962. It consisted of about 9,000 square yards of pasture, filled with small hills, big rocks, and even a swamp, quickly dubbed "the water hole" by Kennedy. Jackie persuaded a hunt-country friend to reduce the wiry grass from about sixteen inches to four inches with a bush hog and in each corner of the pasture they cut small plots down to two inches. These are both the tees and the greens, which require a five iron instead of a putter to negotiate.

I played on this "golf course" with the president when he shot the course record, a thirty-seven for four holes. "It was a pasture for a hundred years," he said, "and it still is."

On this day I teed up trembling at unheard snickers, but managed to hit the longest, straightest goddamn drive of my life ("Jesus, Benjy," the president said, "I never saw anyone hit a ball that far on this hole. You must be hungry"), but it was so far I couldn't find it and Kennedy wouldn't help me look for it. So I lost the first hole. Later in the round I actually sank a five iron, but instead of pausing to relish and to be congratulated (even cheered by the people lining the road?), the president simply picked up his ball and raced to the next tee. It really isn't fair.

Driving back to the Auchincloss house with Tony and Jackie, the president stopped his car to chat with three nuns who were part of a crowd of about 200 people who had been watching us play golf. Kennedy wanted to know all about them, what order they were in, where they worked, etc. They were pouring on the "God loves you's" when we were all startled to hear the president tell the sisters "Jackie here always wanted to be a nun . . . she went to a convent school and really planned to take the orders."

Paul Bunyan rides again

SEPTEMBER 24, 1963 / Except for his love of the sea, John Fitzgerald Kennedy was about the most urban —and urbane—man I have ever met. A well-manicured golf course, perhaps, or an immaculate lawn turned into a touch football field, but that is as far as he could comfortably remove himself from the urban amenities without wondering what the hell he was doing, and worrying that he might make a fool of himself. An outdoorsman he was not. He didn't like to fish, as Eisenhower had. There is one picture of him in feathered headdress posing with some Indians on a reservation, but only one. He didn't like shooting, and he was appalled once when he visited the LBJ Ranch and was taken in a limousine to a carpeted blind to shoot deer that had been driven toward him. He was a product of big-city life, and the comforts and conveniences that his family fortune had provided.

And so his trip across the northern tier of the United States to honor the cause of conservation was

Cruising off the Maine coast on Marietore. "Except for his love of the sea, John Fitzgerald Kennedy was about the most urban—and urbane—man I have ever met. A well-manicured golf course, perhaps, or an immaculate lawn turned into a touch football field, but that is as far as he could comfortably remove himself from the urban amenities without wondering what the hell he was doing, and worrying that he might make a fool of himself. An outdoorsman he was not. . . . He was a product of big-city life, and the comforts and conveniences that his family fortune had provided."

an anomaly from the start. His friends in the press had christened him Paul Bunyan in honor of the occasion, and an unlikelier Paul Bunyan it would be hard to find, in his well-tailored suits, his custom-made shoes and shirts, walking through the fields and mountains of this land, dedicating dams and parklands.

Tony and I had been particularly involved in this trip. I was going along as the *Newsweek* reporter and Tony was going on the first leg of the trip as Kennedy's guest since the president's first stop was to be in Milford, Pennsylvania, the family seat of the Pinchots, where Tony had spent summers as a child, and where her mother, Ruth Pinchot, now lived. The occasion for the presidential visit to Milford was to accept on behalf of the United States the gift of a mansion and some land from Gifford Pinchot, Jr., Tony's first cousin and the son of the late Gifford Pinchot, a former Bull Mooser who had been the first United States Forester and twice governor of Pennsylvania. That in itself was probably not enough to command the president's presence. But a chance to see where his friends the Pinchot girls had grown up, and especially a chance to see their mother, was apparently irresistible.

Ruth Pinchot and John Kennedy had met, even liked each other guardedly. But to say that they were from opposite sides of the political spectrum is putting it mildly. Ruth Pinchot came out of Elmira, New York as a liberal graduate of Elmira Free Academy, but during the later years of Franklin Delano Roosevelt she and her husband turned toward the right, hard right. Her affection for her daughters led her to be more than civil to their friend the president, but it was assumed that every time she saw him, she assuaged her guilt by doubling her contributions to Senator Barry

Goldwater and to William F. Buckley's *National Review* magazine.

Tony and her sister, Mary Meyer, flew from Washington to an air base near Milford, in Newburgh, N.Y., with the president and Secretary of Agriculture Orville Freeman, and to Milford itself in the president's helicopter. I arrived beforehand via the regular press plane. The ceremony and the president's acceptance speech were brief and unnotable. But afterwards, instead of visiting the governor's mansion, which had just been given to the United States, Kennedy insisted on visiting Ruth Pinchot's house—the poor relations' quarters a few hundred yards down the road. I couldn't jostle my way through the crowd, but could only stare in fascination while photographers snapped one of history's most frozen shots . . . the Democratic president surrounded by the arch-Republican mother and her two Democratic daughters.

After Milford, the trek of Paul Bunyan through America had little personal interest, and it never was much of a story.

The president would call my hotel room every few days to chat on the telephone, and once in Jackson Hole, Wyoming, he called to ask me "to a little party we're having later in the evening" after the day's festivities. But Kenny O'Donnell called me later that afternoon to uninvite me, without explanation.

"Maybe now you'll come with us to Texas"
"Sure I will, Jack"

OCTOBER 22, 1963 / I was almost an hour late to dinner with the Kennedys last night. We didn't get asked until almost seven o'clock, and I had a television panel thing to do that I couldn't—and didn't want to —get out of.

The president was in his shirt sleeves when I arrived, and apparently had been telling Jackie and Tony what a miserable day he'd had, with everything going wrong from beginning to end. The latest news involved the refusal of the Birmingham, Alabama, police department to hire Negro cops. Another problem involved Manny Celler (Emmanuel Celler, the New York congressman and chairman of the House Judiciary Committee) and the civil rights bill in the Judiciary Committee, where the liberals were trying to report out a bill which the president feels "gives me a bad bill, and only a fair issue."

Chief topics for discussion tonight were Jackie's recent trip to Greece and a stay on Aristotle Onassis' yacht, and Bobby Baker, the secretary of the Senate majority and a protegé of Lyndon B. Johnson. Baker was under all kinds of investigation and had just been sued, in a civil suit, for taking a bribe in connection with a vending machine franchise in a plant of a company which handled a lot of government contracts.

Kennedy was unwilling to knock Bobby Baker, saying, "I thought of him primarily as a rogue, not a crook. He was always telling me he knew where he could get me the cutest little girls, but he never did. And I found that when I would call him up to get an accurate count on a vote, I'd get a straight answer."

I told Kennedy what *Newsweek* had uncovered and what we were learning from other reporters. The name of Jay McDonald came up, and I identified him as one of our sources. The president said "He's a nice guy, who got really screwed by Bobby" Baker. Kennedy was reluctant to take reports of Baker's sexual adventures too seriously, or the trouble that he might get into as a result of them. I talked about our efforts to find out Baker's net worth and how high the figure was getting, given the fact that he was making a salary of only $19,612. The president interrupted to say "That's where they'll get him . . . on his taxes." Something called "Mansfield Industries" had popped up as a Baker venture, and I wondered if by any chance the name had anything to do with Senator Mike Mansfield, the new majority leader of the Senate and one of the few thoroughly decent human beings ever to serve in Congress. "Mike is a saint. That's all," the president said. "If Mike's involved, then I just give up." (Mansfield was *not* involved in that scandal, or any other one.)

On the question of his vice-president, whose close ties to Baker were politically embarrassing to the Kennedy administration, the president said he felt sure Johnson had not been "on the take since he was elected." Before that, Kennedy said, "I'm not so sure." I asked him about reports *Newsweek* had heard that LBJ was using airplanes supplied to him free by the Grumman Aircraft Corporation. "He's flying on an Air Force jet now," he replied, clearly implying that he, too, had heard about the Grumman planes, but he offered no information or explanation. I told him about some letters *Newsweek* had received anonymously in the mail, from Johnson to Carl Hayden (the senior senator from Arizona, who was president pro tempore of the Senate). "Dear Carl," one of these letters had said, and I was reading from them since I had copies in my pocket, "Every night when I say my prayers I ask the Lord for only one thing . . . twenty more Carl Haydens." The president shuddered, and said that he had received similar letters by the score, "but he only wants one of me."

The president is obviously briefed to his teeth on the Baker case. For instance, he knew that I had called Bobby Kennedy about an incident involving Senator Thomas J. McIntire of New Hampshire, and that Bobby Kennedy had told me the FBI would investigate. (At this time, this story had not appeared in print. *Newsweek* had heard, and later wrote, that Baker had approached McIntire to say that he had heard the senator still had $10,000 outstanding in campaign debts, and to report that he knew "some people" who would be glad to "pick it up" if McIntire were interested. McIntire had declined the offer.) The president is concerned that the deeper the Baker investigation goes, the more Baker and the Southern Democrats will feel that Kennedy is out to get Baker, but more importantly, to get Lyndon Johnson. For instance, he said, the fact that the McIntire-Baker episode will break in *Newsweek* will make everyone believe that he gave me the story, and that will just fan the flames.

"I'm not after Bobby Baker," he repeated, and then talked again about how he felt Baker was more rogue than crook. As for dumping Lyndon Johnson from the ticket in 1964, the president said "That's preposterous on the face of it. We've got to carry Texas in '64, and maybe Georgia."

The Baker conversation put us into a discussion of morality in government generally, and the new, sophisticated immorality, which less often now consists of anything so bold as cash, but rather the hiring of a senator's or a congressman's law firm, for exorbitant fees and no work, or the steering of government business to firms in which elected officials have a financial stake. We talked about taxes and who pays how much. The president stunned us all by saying that J. Paul Getty, the oil zillionaire who was reputedly the richest man in the world, paid exactly $500 in income taxes last year, and that H. L. Hunt, the Texas oil zillionaire who must be one of the next richest, paid only $22,000 in income taxes last year. When I told him that is what Tony and I had paid in taxes last year, he said "The tax laws really screw people in your bracket, buddy boy."

I asked him, since he had obviously done some research on the tax payments of millionaires, how much Daniel Ludwig had paid, referring back to the owner of the yacht that failed to salute the commander-in-chief last month in Newport. He smiled but he didn't bite, and then said that all this tax information was secret, and it was probably illegal for him to know or at least for him to tell me. I told him if he ever wanted to give a tax reform bill the last little push, all he had to do was let me publish this kind of information. He paused, and then said, "Maybe after 1964," a phrase that is cropping up more and more.

On the subject of Onassis, much of the conversation was across the table between Jackie and Tony. There had been substantial press criticism of Jackie's trip. The president had promised it to her as a way of recuperating from the hammer blow of the death of her last child, but the papers had been full of stories about the "brilliantly lighted luxury yacht," "gay with guests, good food and drinks," "lavish shipboard dinners," "dancing music," "a crew of sixty, two coiffeurs, and a dance band." And Republican Congressman Oliver Bolton of Ohio had made a speech on the floor of the House last week criticizing the presence aboard Onassis' yacht of Franklin D. Roosevelt, Jr., who was the under secretary of commerce, and as such was in a position to influence the relations between the Greek shipping tycoon and the U.S. Maritime Administration.

Jackie told us that Onassis "was an alive and vital person" who had started from nothing, who had not wanted to make the trip with Jackie and her sister, Lee Radziwill (and the Roosevelts and Princess Irene Galitzine, the fashion designer, among others). She told us how she had insisted that she would not accept this man's hospitality and then not let him come along. It was an act of kindness, she said. "Poor Franklin didn't want to go along at all," she continued. "He said he was working on a new image and a trip like this wouldn't do him any good, but I persuaded Jack to call Franklin and ask him to go with me. I really wanted him as a chaperon." Jackie seems a little remorseful about all the publicity, including the *Newsweek* story which she felt went a little heavy on hijinks. She said JFK was being "really nice and understanding."

The president did reveal that he had insisted that Onassis now not come to the United States until after 1964, the best evidence that he thinks the trip is potentially damaging to him politically. But he noted that what he called "Jackie's guilt feelings" may work to his advantage.

"Maybe now you'll come with us to Texas next month," he said with a smile.

"And Jackie answered: "Sure I will, Jack."

After exhausting Baker and Onassis as subjects of conversation, we got to that time of the evening when talk jumps from one subject to another with great speed. Jack asked me about my TV panel thing, where I had gotten into a donnybrook with GOP Congressman Tom Curtis from Missouri. "A real bastard," the president announced simply, and Jackie wanted to know when the show would be on the air. She said she liked to watch me on television, but only when I got mad.

On presidential politics, Kennedy now seems to be less sure that the Republicans will nominate Barry Goldwater. He is beginning to believe that the Republicans won't let him have the nomination, though he can't believe they will turn to Nixon again, and he feels he could "really clobber" Nelson Rockefeller this time. "I don't think Barry should try to tackle Rockefeller in New Hampshire," he said. "That's basically a Rockefeller state, and a defeat there would be disastrous for Goldwater." (Goldwater did enter the New Hampshire primary, and ran second to Henry Cabot Lodge.)

Back to morality for another round, we discussed the case of the secretary of the Navy, Fred Korth, who had resigned a week ago. Korth had ostensibly quit over a disagreement with McNamara on the subject of construction of a nuclear-powered aircraft carrier, which McNamara opposed.

Actually Korth had been asked to resign after he had been caught using official Navy stationery for private business purposes. He was a defendant in a civil suit filed some time ago, accused with seven others of conspiring fraudulently to enrich themselves through stock manipulation of the Professional and Business Men's Insurance Co. of Dallas, Texas. Korth and the others had had to turn over some $850,000 worth of stock to an equitable trust. The president said he was convinced it was more a question of stupidity than anything else . . . more unethical than illegal. "He didn't benefit from anything he did," the president said.

As we left, the Kennedys asked us back tomorrow night to see the James Bond movie *From Russia With Love.*

"How many pairs of shoes do you have, George?"

OCTOBER 23, 1963 / Jackie was alone in the living room, going over the financial record of her White House decoration project, when we arrived for dinner. "We're in the red again," she moaned. "The guide books aren't selling as fast as we are making improvements." She disappeared to get dressed and came back in a few minutes wearing the Moroccan caftan that King Moulay Hassan had given her—white silk, with a lot of beautiful embroidery and a stone-studded belt. While we waited for JFK to show up, she talked about the Moroccan part of her recent trip—after she had left Onassis' yacht. She talked about how she had eaten with her hands . . . only one hand, the other is considered impure because of the bodily function it performs, she explained prudishly . . . about the palaces, the Moors, the child dancers she had seen. She put some records of the Moroccan dances on the record player, which is going most of the time during the cocktail hour, and she illustrated some of the bumps and grinds the dancers do.

The president arrived, steaming about the difficulties of doing business with Charlie Halleck, the Indiana congressman who is minority leader of the House of Representatives. "Trying to touch Charlie is like trying to pick up a greased pig," he said. He had just finished an hour and forty-five minutes with Halleck, Les Arends (the Illinois Republican who was the House GOP whip), Speaker McCormack, and some other congressional leaders, trying to find a way out of the civil rights impasse. "It's a lousy bill as it now stands," he announced. "One section of the bill that requires the collection of some statistics would cost $95 million a year, according to the Budget Bureau. The bill as it now stands would gut the voting rights section," he said, because it provides for appeals that could take three or four years to litigate, and the public accommodations section includes everything from school to barber shops. He is obviously preoccupied with this problem. He took a call from Burke Marshall, the assistant attorney general in charge of the civil rights division of the Justice Department, and asked Marshall to collect all the statements he could find from Negro leaders like Roy Wilkins, head of the NAACP, and James Farmer, national director of CORE, praising the original bill submitted to Congress by the Kennedy administration.

Jim Bishop, the writer who specializes in recreating historic days, and his wife had been in the White House all day, researching a story for *Reader's Digest* on a day in the life of the Kennedys. The president wanted to know what questions they had asked Jackie and her maid, Provie, and exactly what answers they'd given. Jackie quoted Provie as saying that the Bishops had wanted to know what Mrs. Kennedy wore to bed, and who slept where. Kennedy seemed to be relieved when Jackie reported that Provie had been uncommunicative on that particular subject. Jackie described her session with the Bishops as chaotic, with one dog biting the other, with the children shouting and screaming up a storm, and with the telephone buzzing like mad. She said Bishop had told her everyone in the White House referred to Dave Powers as "John's Other Wife," but the president didn't seem to think that was very funny.

The president regaled everyone by reporting what George Thomas, his valet, had volunteered to the Bishops. Bishop had apparently asked George how many pairs of shoes the president owned. Imitating George, hemming as he puts his eyes to the ceiling, Kennedy said "about twenty-five." He apparently had chewed George out pretty good for releasing this bit of information, asking him if he didn't understand the political implications of such splendor. "How many pairs of shoes do you own, George?" he said he had asked his valet. "One," George had replied. "Well," Kennedy had countered, "don't you see how most of the people who own only one pair of shoes might resent my having twenty-five . . . even if it were true?" We asked him how many pairs of shoes he did in fact own, and he said he had no idea.

A similar exaggeration—if in fact it is an exaggeration—occurred when Bishop asked George about how many times a day the president changed his shirt. George had apparently replied "six," and this truly bugged the fashion-plate president. When we asked him what the right answer for today was, damned if it wasn't four. He said he'd started the day off with one clean shirt, put on another after his swim before a lunch honoring the Bolivian president Dr. Victor Paz Estenssoro, donned a third after the lunch because it had been so hot during the lunch, and just now he had put on his fourth clean shirt after a bath before dinner. He was shocked and disapproving when I told him I sometimes wore the same shirt two days in a row, especially in winter.

Jackie said she felt the Bishops were prying awfully deep into their privacy, but Kennedy said "Never mind. It's the lead story in *Reader's Digest*, and the way things are going for us right now, we can use anything we get. Anyway, we have the right of clearance." And after a pause: "That's a great thing, that right of clearance."

The Bobby Baker case came up again when JFK mentioned that the *Post* had run a picture of Baker's house this morning. I told him how I had heard that when *Time* had rung the doorbell at the house at 9:00 A.M. the other morning, they were greeted by two women in evening dresses. "Did they get the picture?" Kennedy wanted to know immediately. I told him one of the women was reportedly a hostess on the Pan American charter plane that ferried the press around on presidential journeys. "What's her name?" he asked again, but I couldn't help him.

At dinner we got talking about Dean Acheson. The president had apparently called him that afternoon to get a report on Acheson's recent trip to Germany. "I think Acheson . . . and Clark Clifford in a different way," the president said out of the blue, "are the two best advocates I have ever heard. Acheson would have made a helluva Supreme Court justice, although he was sixty-seven or sixty-eight when I had my first vacancy." The president implied that was too old for a Supreme Court justice, at least to be appointed by him.

Evidently quoting Acheson, Kennedy wondered aloud about how Adenauer could still be steaming— at the age of eighty-eight—about being shunted aside. He told a story about how Ludwig Erhard, Adenauer's successor, had gone to see Adenauer after delivering a two-hour inaugural address. Apparently Adenauer had greeted him by saying "You're only going to be in office two years, and you took almost that long to say what you were going to do." The Germans are just different from everyone else, Kennedy quoted Acheson as saying, and you have to treat them differently from everyone else.

Kennedy said he thought the appointment of Lord Alec Douglas-Home to be the new British prime minister was first-class. All the others were old hat, and the younger ones, Reginald Maudling and Edward Heath, were both unmarried and in their forties, a condition which he apparently felt disqualified them. "Macmillan did the right thing in not appointing either one," he said. As soon as he had mentioned Macmillan's name, Jackie asked him to tell us the story about the British prime minister and Richard Nixon. Kennedy said that Macmillan had once told him that Eisenhower had said of Nixon "I wouldn't have him on the place." We all agreed that this was the language of the lordly Macmillan, even if the thought had been President Eisenhower's. The phrase was apparently used when Eisenhower was telling Macmillan how badly Nixon had once wanted to spend a weekend at Camp David, and Eisenhower had refused to let him.

Kennedy found the deceptive Harold Macmillan

"Kennedy found the deceptive Harold Macmillan a true delight, primarily because he made the president laugh at his troubles, which was the truest way to Kennedy's affection. . . . Just one month after the Bay of Pigs, Kennedy said Macmillan had greeted him by saying, 'I could really have performed my ultimate service to mankind if those Cubans would only have shot down my plane; then you could have had your little invasion.'"

a true delight, primarily because he made the president laugh at his troubles, which was the truest way to Kennedy's affection. Whenever he had been in any kind of contact with the British prime minister, Kennedy came away with an anecdote or two that pleased him enormously. My favorite involved a cruise Kennedy and Macmillan were taking down the Potomac on the *Honey Fitz* after a working day of discussions about their mutual problems—one of which was the tiny, artificial country of Laos. As the yacht steamed south on the Potomac, the two free-world leaders were sitting on the fantail when they pulled alongside a small flotilla of eight-oared shells from a local high school in their regular late afternoon practice.

"Ah, what have we here?" Kennedy quoted Macmillan as saying. "Looks like the Laotian navy," a reference to the legendary unwillingness of the Laotians to fight as fiercely as the Anglo-American policy would have them fight.

Macmillan had instinctively understood the surest way to Kennedy's affection and esteem . . . by leavening serious, knowledgeable discussion with humor and style, and the two leaders had hit it off ever since their first meeting in Nassau. At that time, just one month after the Bay of Pigs, Kennedy said Macmillan had greeted him by saying "I could really have performed my ultimate service to mankind if those Cubans would only have shot down my plane; then you could have had your little invasion."

Discussion of Nixon led us to the question of vice-presidents in general. "The steam really went out of Lyndon, didn't it," the president noted, "when they wouldn't let him into the party caucus."

And LBJ led us to a discussion of 1968 and the question of whom Kennedy might try to crown as his successor. The thought—and sound—of Kennedy nominating Johnson . . . "I'd go to the well with that man," done in Kennedy broad-A . . . brought a few smiles. We were walking down to the movie theater when Jackie came back to the subject by asking "Well, then who?" The president said, "It was going to be Franklin, until you and Onassis fixed that," but there was no edge in his voice.

The movie was James Bond, and Kennedy seemed to enjoy the cool and the sex and the brutality. Ethel and Bobby were there waiting in the theater, the attorney general dressed like a Brooks Brothers beatnik. He borrowed a buck from me to buy papers on the way home.

Tony reported later that during one discussion Jackie had reported on her latest turn as the cooperative mother at Marina's and John-John's nursery school that day. She had been appalled that she had to help the little boys go to the bathroom.

As we left, Kennedy said again that they were definitely now going out west for the 1964 summer vacation. "To Montana," he said, "not to those cold bastards in Wyoming."

"Boy, the dirt he has on those senators"

NOVEMBER 5, 1963 / Evelyn Lincoln called us after 6:00 P.M. with an invitation to dinner at eight with the Kennedys. We begged off because we were giving a cocktail party for *Newsweek*'s foreign editor, Bob Christopher. Evelyn asked us if we could make it at 8:30, and we did.

J. Edgar Hoover, the FBI chief, had been to lunch with Kennedy a few days before, and Kennedy was full of that meeting. He told us how FDR used to have Hoover over regularly, and said he felt it was wise for him to start doing the same thing, with rumors flying and every indication of a dirty campaign coming up. "Boy, the dirt he has on those senators," Kennedy said, shaking his head. "You wouldn't believe it." He described a picture of Elly Rometsch that Hover had brought him. Her name had popped up in and out of print as one of the women who frequented the Quorum Club, Bobby Baker's relaxing emporium on Capitol Hill. The FBI had been telling its newspaper friends that she was often in and out of Baker's Washington home and the Carousel Motel, which Baker owned, on the Maryland seashore. She and her husband, a German air force sergeant, were returned to Germany a few months ago after the FBI and German intelligence officials had checked on her swinging activities. Kennedy said the picture showed her to be "a really beautiful woman." Hoover told Kennedy at lunch that his agents had obtained an affidavit from Elly Rometsch in West Germany stating that she wanted to return to the United States, not to go back in business, but to marry the chief investigator of a Senate committee, whom Kennedy knew. This man, Kennedy quoted Hoover as saying, "was getting for free what Elly was charging others a couple of hundred dollars a night." Apparently at least one more German girl was involved in what Hoover called "this ring," a girl who had also left the country, but not by invitation of the U.S. government. There is something incredible about the picture of the president of the United States and the director of the Federal Bureau of Investigation looking at photographs of call girls over lunch in the White House living quarters.

We were into morals and ethics in government now, and that brought us pretty quickly to Bobby Baker once more. Kennedy wondered whether "you all"—not the Justice Department, interestingly—will get Baker on anything except conflict of interest. He told us a story —which Edward Bennett Williams, who was Baker's lawyer, had told me a few days ago—involving Congressman Torby MacDonald and a small-time "rain-maker" around town named Mickey Weiner. A rain-maker is a Washington operator who claims to be able to make it rain right for his client in the jungle of government. (In 1964, during the Senate investigation of Baker, Weiner was questioned about a $5,000 payment he made to Baker for "legal fees" after a client's bill had been enacted into law. Weiner told an incredulous committee that he had wasted his money, since Baker had done nothing to help the bill pass.) Apparently the FBI got to Weiner for questioning in Palm Springs, California, and who should be with him but Torby MacDonald, the Massachusetts congressman and Kennedy's longtime friend. The president heard about it, I suppose, within a few seconds—and reached Torby on the telephone. "What the hell are you doing in the company of a guy like Mickey Weiner?" the president said he asked MacDonald. Torby said he was in Palm Springs to make a speech and had bumped into Weiner, about whom he knew very little. "Don't you know he's a friend of Bobby's?" Kennedy said he asked MacDonald, meaning a friend of Bobby Baker. "That's good, isn't it?" Torby replied, thinking the president had meant a friend of Bobby Kennedy. "Bobby Baker, you dope," the president replied.

We speculated on who would be a good independent counsel to conduct the Senate investigation into the Baker case, an independent man without disqualifying ties to any of the people involved. "Whizzer White, if he weren't on the Supreme Court," the president suggested. "Or Clark Clifford, if he weren't my friend."

We speculated, too, on who might be the hidden Profumo in the Kennedy administration. Kennedy had devoured every word written about the Profumo case; it combined so many of the things that interested him: low doings in high places, the British nobility, sex, and spying. Someone in the State Department had apparently sent him an early cable on the Profumo case from David Bruce, the American ambassador to Great Britain. Kennedy had been so fascinated by that cable that he had ordered all further cables from Bruce on that subject sent to him immediately. "His cables are just fantastic," the president reported. "He writes so damn well, full of insights about our British friends."

Pierre Salinger, we guessed, might be the people's choice as a likely American Profumo, but not with us. Bill Henry (Federal Communications Commission chairman William Henry) got a call, as did Roz Gilpatric (Rozwell Gilpatric, under secretary of defense). Kennedy told us that Jackie thought Gilpatric was "the second most attractive" man in the Defense Department. The first was obviously Bob McNamara. "Men can't understand his sex appeal," Jackie said. "Look at them," she said to Tony, pointing to Kennedy and me. "They look just like dogs that have had a plate of food grabbed from under their noses."

We got back to the question of ethics among congressmen—and especially senators. "Look at Estes Kefauver and his $300,000, for God's sake," the president exclaimed, referring to the surprisingly large estate the late Tennessee senator had left. "What can you say about that?" Charlie Bartlett had written him a letter, the president said, urging him to find a job for Nancy Kefauver because she was broke. Kennedy said he had found her a job selecting art to hang in U.S. embassies abroad, and then Charlie had written him another letter apologizing, saying he'd been embarrassed to learn than Kefauver had left an estate of $300,000, including substantial holdings of stocks in some drug companies that he had been investigating.

This was election night, and throughout the evening the president received telephone calls briefing him on the results, particularly in Philadelphia and in Kentucky. (It was also autobahn night. A few minutes before we arrived for dinner, an allied convoy which had been blocked for two days got through to Berlin.) Kennedy was not wildly enthusiastic about the election returns, but at one point conceded "The way things have been going, to win in Philadelphia, Kentucky, and the autobahn adds up to a pretty good day."

As usual, the president had a good deal to say about *Newsweek* and the *Washington Post*. He was particularly critical of a *Newsweek* piece last week about civil rights. He claimed we had some dates wrong, which had made the import of the whole story wrong. I didn't have the details to rebut him, if there are any. On the subject of the *Post*, he said there had been "a noticeable deterioration" in the paper since Phil Graham's death. As we argued out this outlandish statement, it turned out to mean in translation that he felt the *Post* had been considerably tougher on him in the last few months.

Kennedy asked me if it was true that *Newsweek* was preparing a "very critical" cover story on John A. McCone, who had succeeded Allen Dulles as head of the Central Intelligence Agency. This was the same question he had asked Pierre Salinger to ask Chuck Roberts, our White House correspondent, earlier that day. His particular interest in this story fascinated me, and bugged me a bit, and I asked him how come he was so involved. Somehow McCone had told Hoover, who had told Bobby, who had told the president, and I felt slightly pressured, especially since the status of the McCone cover story is *quo ante,* unwritten, and only imprecisely planned.

The president reported that he had decided not to mention Barry Goldwater's name again in his public appearances. He said he hoped it would be Goldwater that he ran against, because "I really like him, and if we're licked at least it will be on the issues. At least the people will have a clear choice." He noted that the Arizona senator had had a bad week for a presidential candidate. He found it unbelievable that Goldwater had written a Tennessee Democrat a letter saying that if he were president he would sell the Tennessee Valley Authority to private business. "You just don't write that kind of thing, first of all, and certainly not to someone not in your party." That letter should have been answered by some secretary way down the line, he said. I had just done a Q and A interview with Goldwater, which Kennedy said "was fantastic . . . especially the part about when Barry called up and changed his vote." The president really reads the fine print; the last paragraph of the Goldwater interview read "Goldwater was asked why he had voted for the six billion dollar appropriation bill late last month, after he had ceaselessly called for 'a prompt and final termination of the farm subsidy program.' Goldwater denied that he had done so. When he was shown that he had been paired for the bill, he called the clerk of the Senate and had his vote changed to 'No.'"

For some reason, our inability to get our daughter Nancy into dancing school came up again. It's really formidable to see the pleasure the president gets out of this story. It's almost as if he were getting even for all those "No Irish Need Apply" signs with which he thinks my Bradlee ancestors tucked it to his Kennedy-Fitzgerald ancestors. He repeats all the advice "that Dad would have given and followed," namely to get out of town rather than take this social snub, and throws his head back and roars with laughter. He said he told the story to lots of people, including his brother-in-law, Peter Lawford, "who hasn't had a very good week himself (referring to reports that Lawford and Pat Kennedy Lawford were splitting up)." Kennedy offered to bet me a hundred dollars that Tony and I couldn't get ourselves asked to something called the Dancing Class, a snobby subscription dance in town. I'd pay more than that to stay away from the Dancing Class, but I'm intrigued by the prospect of taking the hundred off him.

Somehow we got on the subject of people in the administration who had gotten swelled heads as a result of their association with the New Frontier. Jackie said there were only two by her count: Dick Donahue (Richard Donahue, an assistant to Larry O'Brien in the legislative liaison operation), and Jack McNally, who worked in a low-level job in the White House transportation division. Kennedy defended Donahue strongly, and dismissed McNally with a flick of his finger. Donahue was leaving, he said, because he had eight children and simply had to go out and earn some money. I reminded Kennedy that Donahue was the man whom Teddy White had described as "coruscatingly brilliant" in his book on the 1960 election. Kennedy laughed and said, "Sometimes these guys forget that fifty thousand votes the other way and they'd all be coruscatingly stupid."

The president asked innocently what *Newsweek* would have on the cover next week, but it turned out that he already knew. The cover was on smoking, to coincide with the surgeon general's long-awaited report. Bobby had told him of our plans, and told him the cover story was going to be "critical." I told him we had had great difficulty with this cover since the secrets were so tightly held, and the president told us that we must have had some success, because we had succeeded in getting one man fired because he had talked to us. The report was so secret, Kennedy said, that even his scientific advisor, Jerry Weisner, had been unable to see it or involve himself in the deliberations that led to the surgeon general's conclusions. The president went over all the difficulties they'd had with the report, the enormous importance of tobacco to the economics of several states and to the national revenue. He asked me what the evidence would be on how much more likely a smoker was to get cancer than a non-smoker. This evening he - chain-smoked three cigars, once lighting one from another.

The president had been upset this morning by a picture on the front page of the *Post* showing some GIs dancing with prostitutes in Saigon. As soon as he had seen it, he said he had called Bob Manning at the State Department to say that it was a "put-up job" by the Associated Press, and to ask Manning to do something about it. "If I were running things in Saigon," he said, "I'd have those GIs in the front line the next morning."

Kennedy revealed that he had seen Cord Meyer, Tony's former brother-in-law, now high in the CIA, recently about the Dominican Republic. What about the Dominican Republic? I asked. It turns out the question under discussion was "whether or not to have a student demonstration down there." The president seemed unconcerned about the morality of the secret intelligence arm of the U.S. government staging a phony demonstration in a foreign country to further American policy objectives. I asked him about how we would feel if the Soviet Union staged demonstrations in America this callously to further their objectives, but got no answer.

Before we left we reminisced about the night of the West Virginia primary, the dirty movie we had seen, whose plot the president seemed to recall remarkably well given his preoccupations that night. And we discussed plans for this weekend in Atoka, our first trip to the new Virginia pad, and the first weekend the president will have spent the night in his new house.

"You're about to see a president trampled to death by a horse"

NOVEMBER 10, 1963 / "Wexford" is the name Jackie has given to the new Kennedy weekend digs in the rolling countryside west of Middleburg, Virginia. I won my bet with the president about the cost . . . something over $100,000, they admit, but he shows no signs of paying me. It's a fancy, one-story rambler, finished in stucco, very swell, with a stable and a Secret Service "facility" off to one side, half hidden in the woods. It has an unlived-in decorator look, but then it hasn't been lived in.

It was a cool, sunny fall day, but still warm enough to have Bloody Marys outside on the terrace, sitting on a stone wall overlooking fields and a new, muddy man-made pond. Caroline's pony, Macaroni, was loose on the terrace and contributed to a scene that had us laughing so hard our stomachs ached. We were leaning against the side of the house, out of the wind in order

CECIL STOUGHTON PHOTO
Ben Bradlee and John-John that last weekend in Virginia.

"It was a cool, sunny fall day, but still warm enough to have Bloody Marys outside on the terrace, sitting on a stone wall overlooking fields and a new, muddy, man-made pond. . . . At dinner we talked about his trip next week to Florida, and the trip the week after to Texas. . . . We left in the middle of the next day, after another relaxed morning, watching Jackie ride and jump, walking and reading the papers.

"It was the last time I ever saw him."

to get the full sun. Major Cecil Stoughton, the White House photographer, was milling around still snapping pictures after a morning taking shots of Jackie riding Sardar, the Arabian stallion given to her by Ayub Khan, president of Pakistan. All of a sudden the pony walked onto the front lawn, munching grass, oblivious to us all. He kept getting closer and closer, until the rest of us got up and scattered, but the president sat there, pretending to be fearless. Macaroni finally got so close to Kennedy that his nose was actually nudging the presidential rear end as he nibbled grass. And he wouldn't stop, pushing JFK over on his side, and then onto his stomach, and then onto his other side, in his search for more and more grass. We were getting hysterical, and the president was shouting to Stoughton, "Are you getting this, Captain? You're about to see a president trampled to death by a horse." (Stoughton got the pictures on eight mm. movie film. They appeared much later in *Look* magazine, and still later in the book *A Very Special President* by *Look* photographer Stanley Tretick and writer Laura Bergquist.) We spent the afternoon sitting on the stone wall reading the papers, and walking through the fields.

At dinner we talked about his trip next week to Florida, and the trip the week after to Texas. Florida was presenting no particular political problems, but the political situation in Texas was fouled up, with Governor John Connally feuding with Senator Ralph Yarborough, and with Vice-President Lyndon Johnson a less viable mediator than he had once been. And the mood of the city was ugly; a month before, UN Ambassador Adlai Stevenson had been booed, jeered, hit with signs, and spat upon at a United Nations Day rally.

Texas brought us to Bobby Baker—again—and

Baker's name prompted the president to suggest an elaborate practical joke. Kennedy suggested that I call Torby MacDonald, without saying where I was, and tell him that the story about the FBI questioning of Mickey Weiner was surfacing, and with it the fact that the FBI had found Weiner with MacDonald in Palm Springs, and that I was afraid that I was going to have to write a small story about the whole thing. "Lay it on old Torb good" he urged, with almost childish anticipation. The Signal Corps operators, who worked all Kennedy country retreats, got the congressman promptly, and I laid it on him good, with the president and Jackie listening on an extension.

"Listen, Torb," I began, "I'm afraid I've got a problem, and I'm afraid it's a problem that's going to involve you." Torby's enthusiasm waned audibly.

Bradlee: "You know that time when the FBI questioned Mickey Weiner about his role in the Bobby Baker case, and you were with him in Palm Springs?"

MacDonald: "Yeah. Well, what about it?"

Bradlee: "Well, the story's getting around, and I'm afraid I'm going to have to write a piece about it. You know the Baker case is big news, and Weiner is involved, and what I have to know is what your connection with all of it is. What your connection is with Weiner."

MacDonald: "Jesus, I've got no connection with Weiner. I just met him in the hotel where I was giving a speech and he sidled up to me and we talked, that's all."

Kennedy, with hand over mouthpiece: "Torb's hurting. Tuck it to him some more."

Bradlee, imagination now out of control: "Well, the FBI is telling us that there were some girls involved."

MacDonald: "What the hell do you mean, girls?"

Bradlee: "You know, girls, women?"

Kennedy was now slumped over on his back on the sofa, he was laughing so hard.

MacDonald: "I just barely know Weiner, for Christ's sake. What do you have to bring me into this for?"

Bradlee: "Well, you know everyone knows I'm a friend of Jack's and so I've got to be extra careful about anything that involves a friend of his. You know, if we don't write about you and Weiner and the girls, then people will say I'm on the Kennedy payroll, or something like that. So I'm afraid we really have to write something."

At this point the president, posing as me, asked a question of MacDonald, but there was something suspicious about the voice. MacDonald mumbled something, and Kennedy came on with another, meaner question, which I can't remember, but this time in his own voice.

"Oh shit," said the congressman from Massachusetts as he realized he'd been had, and by whom. I never heard Kennedy laugh harder than he did that night.

Late in the evening Pat Lawford showed up, looking very upset and nervous. Jackie and she stayed up literally all night talking, while the rest of us went off to bed.

We left in the middle of the next day, after another relaxed morning watching Jackie ride and jump, walking, and reading the papers.

It was the last time I ever saw him.

Epilogue

NOVEMBER 23, 1963 / The sledgehammer news that President Kennedy had been shot came to me while I was browsing through Brentano's book store on my lunch hour. (It is noteworthy, I think, that virtually everyone I know under sixty can remember exactly where he or she was when the news of the assassination struck them.) First it was the barely distinguishable whispers of incredulous pedestrians, then all too finally it was the AP ticker in the *Newsweek* bureau on the twelfth floor of the National Press Building around the corner. It's not enough to say that you can't believe these terrible things as they happen. I remember savaging a well-meaning *Newsweek* reporter, Dave Burnham, when he pointed to the first bulletins of the assassination and told me, "He's going to die, Ben. He's going to die." Irrationally I turned on him and said "I know goddamn well he's going to die. Just don't gloat about it." Of course he wasn't gloating; he was just retreating into a semblance of professionalism to hide his own shock. And our profession does have that virtue—such as it may be. Disaster, even personal disaster, generally means work to be done, mountains to be moved.

In this case, disaster had struck on a Friday—only twenty-four hours before *Newsweek*'s regular deadline, and mountains had to be moved fast, far closer to the daily newspaper timetable than weekly newsmagazines normally get. After calling Tony, conferring with *News-*

week editors in New York, sending more reporters down to dreadful Dallas, I went into my own office to try to collect my thoughts. I wanted desperately to write something, but I was trembling inside and out, and I didn't know if I could write, much less what I would write. It had to be a tribute, not an obituary, for I realized in a flash that I knew so little of the building blocks that biography demands, only the cement that binds those blocks. It had to be personal, for I also understood that personal insights into this man were all that I could offer that a hundred others couldn't do better. But it couldn't be first person singular; it couldn't overtly, even suggestively, boast of my special access. I remember as if it were yesterday typing, hesitantly, a tentative lead: "America lost a wonderfully warm and graceful and promising President in Dallas last week, and I lost a friend," then ripping it out of the typewriter and shouting at the top of my lungs "Take yourself out of it, you pompous ass!" Off and on during the next twenty hours I worked on this piece, interrupted by two visits to the White House, a ghastly eight-hour vigil at Bethesda Naval Hospital, and the endless interruptions of deadline journalism. It appeared, after the kindest and most understanding editing by Oz Elliott and *Newsweek*'s managing editor, Gordon Manning, under the title "That Special Grace."

Late in the afternoon Nancy Tuckerman, who was Jackie's social secretary, called to ask Tony and me to come to the White House. She said she didn't know where Jackie would go when she returned to Washington, and she didn't know whether Jackie would want to see anyone, but she wanted us standing by. We got there about 6:30, overcome this time by a cheerless dread instead of the exciting gaiety that was the hallmark of other visits. Jean Kennedy Smith was there, Nancy Tuckerman, and later Eunice Kennedy Shriver. There were no tears, only an embarrassed, sad, and stilted silence. About 9:00 Nancy Tuckerman told us that Jackie—and everyone connected with the slain president—were going directly from Andrews Air Force Base, where Air Force One with the new president aboard would land, to Bethesda Naval Hospital. A final autopsy on the president's body would be performed there, and Jackie was apparently determined to stay as close as she could for as long as she could. We went quickly but not silently in a White House limousine to the hospital, accompanied by the senseless screaming sirens of a motorcycle escort splitting the night. Halfway out there we watched in horror as one of the motorcycles spun out of control and we thought surely we would have to add another fatality to this dreadful day, but a miracle brought the rider through, and we begged our driver to slow down.

The next seven hours have stayed blurred in my mind for all these years, except for the moments right after Jackie entered the hospital suite on the arms of the Irish Mafia in the form of Larry O'Brien and Kenny O'Donnell, men she had never really understood or appreciated, but to whom she turned and clung now, strong men from the Irish political side of the dichotomous Kennedy whom Jackie had never met on equal terms, but who now seemed to comfort her more than any of the rest of us. Her entrance, announced to us by the flashes of photographers' bulbs many stories below us, into that dreary hospital green room is scarred on my soul for the rest of my life. Her pink wool suit was copiously spattered with the blood of her dead husband, when she had cradled his shattered head in her lap. She looked so lovely, I remember thinking incongruously. But a closer look showed her to be dazed, moving ever so slowly, with her eyes apparently not taking all of us in. We all rose, stricken and uncomfortable, as she came slowly toward us. When she got to Tony and me her eyes brightened a little, she raised her arms and then lurched into my arms, and sobbed. After a minute or so she pulled back and greeted Tony in the same way. Then she turned to me and said, "Oh Benny, do you want to hear what happened?" And then quickly added, "But not as a reporter for *Newsweek*, okay?" I felt badly that she obviously felt she had to be that careful in that awful moment about the old problem, and was about to proclaim my innocence as usual, when she started telling us of the actual shooting. I can remember now only the strangely graceful arc she described with her right arm as she told us that part of the president's head had been blown away by one bullet. She moved in a trance to talk to each of us there and to new friends as they arrived, ignoring the advice of friends and doctors to get some sleep and to change out of her bloody clothes. Those were some kind of dreadful badge of the disaster she had been through, and no one could persuade her to remove them.

There was an almost silent discussion between Jackie and Kenny O'Donnell about her wedding ring. Apparently she had removed it and placed it in Kennedy's casket, and now had decided she wanted to keep it. Bobby Kennedy, looking exhausted but already clearly emerging as the strongest of the stricken, asked several of us where we thought the president should be buried. There was some sentiment—especially among JFK's early Massachusetts associates—for Boston, but Bobby was coming down on the side of Arlington National

Cemetery. He told us that Bob McNamara had already looked for—and found—the site that was eventually selected. Everyone I heard him ask agreed.

It was past five o'clock in the morning when we left the hospital, after Jackie was finally persuaded to try to get some sleep in one of the bedrooms in the hospital suite.

I was back at the office trying to finish my piece when a call came from the White House asking if we could be over there in an hour for a special private service for family and friends, and the long pageant of mourning was under way, an uneasy mixture of private grief and public sorrow. Kneeling on the bare floor of the East Room, I felt the futility of grief as personal and selfish and useless. There was nothing useful that Tony or I could do, except show up and be counted among the mourners, and that was frustrating. Thankfully, I did have an article to finish, and I did that after we left the White House, and did what I could to make that issue of the magazine as distinguished as possible.

After dinner Saturday night, Jackie telephoned and asked us to join a bunch of friends at the White House, to take her mind off death and funerals. When we got there Dave Powers, that irrepressible veteran of a hundred wakes, who knew instinctively how to comfort families of the dead better than all of us put together, was finally making Jackie laugh, with one story after another about the "three-deckers" in Charlestown, which Dave pronounced "Char-less-town," where he had first met John F. Kennedy. A "three-decker" is a three-story tenement with stairs going up from one outside rear porch to another, and Dave had climbed most of them in his district with JFK. Dave's stories would be interrupted by moments of silence as the television set caught our attention, especially Jackie's attention, with shots of the country grieving, of people, including herself and her children and other Kennedys, filing silently, prayerfully past the presidential casket on view in the halls of Congress.

Jackie was extraordinary. Sometimes she seemed completely detached, as if she were someone else watching the ceremony of that other person's grief. Sometimes she was silent, obviously torn. Often she would turn to a friend and reminisce, and everyone would join in with their remembrance of things forever past. There is much to be said for the wake. Led by Dave Powers, this one was more often than not surprisingly cheerful, and always warm and tender.

CECIL STOUGHTON PHOTO

INDEX

INDEX

248

INDEX

INDEX

INDEX

INDEX

INDEX

The Author

AT THE TIME his conversations with Kennedy took place, Benjamin Bradlee was the Washington bureau chief for *Newsweek* magazine. He has been with the *Washington Post* since 1965 and has been executive editor since 1968. Born in Boston and a Harvard graduate, he has been a journalist except for service in the Navy in World War II and a tour as press attaché at the embassy in Paris from 1951–1953. He was European correspondent for *Newsweek* from 1953–1957.